Exploring Spirituality

Inspiring, informative books for thoughtful readers wanting to make changes and realise their potential.

Other titles in the series include:

Living the Life You Want
Your personal key to true abundance and richness of everyday experience

Dating, Mating & Relating
The complete guide to finding and keeping your ideal partner

Choosing a Better Life
An inspiring step-by-step guide to building the future you want

When What You've Got Is Not What You Want
Use NLP to create the life you want and live it to the full

Healing the Hurt Within
Understand and relieve the suffering behind self-destructive behaviour

Trusting Your Intuition
Rediscover your true self to achieve a richer, more rewarding life

Please send for a free copy of the catalogue for full details
(see back cover for address).

Exploring Spirituality

A step-by-step guide to finding and following your own spiritual path

Suzanne Ruthven and Aeron Medbh-Mara

Pathways

First published in 2001 by
How To Books Ltd, 3 Newtec Place,
Magdalen Road, Oxford OX4 1RE, United Kingdom
Tel: 01865 793806   Fax: 01865 248780

British Library Cataloguing in Publication Data
A catalogue record for this book is available from
the British Library

Edited by Diana Brueton
Cover design by Shireen Nathoo Design

Produced for How To Books by Deer Park Productions
Typeset by Anneset, Weston-super-Mare, Somerset
Printed by Bell and Bain Ltd., Glasgow

Note: The material contained in this book is set out in good
faith for general guidance and no liability can be accepted for loss or expense
incurred as a result of relying in particular circumstances on statements made in
the book. Laws and regulations are complex and liable to change, and readers
should check the current position with the relevant authorities before making
personal arrangements.

Pathways is an imprint of
How To Books

Contents

Introduction

This is not a book about religion. It's a book about *you*.

Exploring Spirituality is a unique step-by-step guide that does not extol the virtues of one particular faith or religion as the definitive guide to an individual's spiritual salvation. Rather, it advocates approaching spirituality as something completely separate from religious belief, seeing them as often being different sides of the same coin. A highly spiritual person may often have no strong religious commitment to any particular faith, while a staunch 'worshipper' can be devoid of any spirituality. As many people have found, religion can be taught but spirituality must be discovered and developed within one's self.

The present social climate has seen a decline in both traditional religious and spiritual values. This has led, in turn, to an increasing number of people seeking salvation in an assortment of alternative religions, Eastern philosophies and mysticism, not to mention the various cults which cast their nets in the direction of the emotionally and spiritually insecure. Moving the goal-post, however, does not necessarily solve the problem and the seeker, more often than not, merely manages to leave themselves even more confused or spiritually damaged.

Spirituality is how we 'feel' about the meaning or mysteries of life; how we reconcile life's highs and lows; where we feel the soul comes from, how it grows and where it goes after death. It addresses the quest for the 'hidden meaning of life' and need not manifest itself in a religious manner – after all, secular spirituality spawned philosophy. Spirituality emphasises ethics over morality.

Religion is *supposed* to be how individual spirituality manifests in public – it is how society interacts, how two or more individuals may exchange information on spiritual matters. Its 'magic' is that of divine intercession, i.e. we ask God to do something for us. It requires the individual to submit to the will of their deity and the

hierarchy of its priesthood, although its function is civic and
motivated towards the need of society and/or state. Religion
emphasises morality over ethics.

Although we now live in a multi-cultural society, the majority
of the population was born and bred under the influence of the
traditional family faith – whether it be Christian, Hindu, Islam or
Judaism. Regular observance of the family faith is a constant
affirmation of ethnic tradition and a bonding together with those
of 'our own kind' to preserve cultural identities. By gathering
together in temple, church, chapel, cathedral, synagogue or
mosque, the adherents of that faith are interacting with other
members of their community under the banner of their religion.

This interaction is reinforced with the cycle of the different rites
of passage, from birth to death, which form the basis for all
community religion. A rite of passage marks the transition within
a person's life, either voluntarily or not, from one state of being to
another. Birth, puberty, menopause and death are all non-
voluntary; voluntary rites are marriage and child-bearing – with
most of these transitions directly affecting other people. Some
religions place a higher level of importance on certain rites than
on others. Some are more orthodox in their approach or
interpretation of the doctrine of their faith, but it is the continual
observance of the rituals and celebrations that maintain the
strength and continuity of the religion within the community.

It is perfectly possible to perceive one's self as a spiritual being
without being at all religious. And it is equally possible to be
religious without developing spirituality. A person can regularly
attend a place of worship and observe all the prescribed rituals in
the religious calendar, but it does not necessarily mean that they
are 'plugged in' to the Divine. After all, many people join a
religious group merely because they are looking for 'something' to
fill a gap in their lives on a social level.

The seeker should bear in mind that those contributing their
thoughts and experiences to *Exploring Spirituality* are not of any
one particular faith. This information has been deliberately
excluded since spirituality is universally recognisable, rendering
such labels superfluous. In this context the use of the term priest,
priestess or priesthood is used to cover all denominations and
faiths rather than the clerical titles normally associated with a
particular religion.

This exploration of spirituality should be likened to starting a diet. To successfully lose weight we need to shed the excess body fat before concentrating on firming up the muscles. In the first part of this book we will be focusing our attention on the mind and body before attending to the needs of the spirit. We need to understand why we have the need to seek answers – and what we're going to do when we receive them.

The authors are both experienced trainers with Pathfinders, a non-religious counselling group which takes a realistic view of why people need to seek something deeper within themselves, and encourages them to understand that 'swapping religion' isn't always the answer. They have both written numerous books on esoteric teaching and spirituality.

CHAPTER 1

Discovering Yourself

'There is an old adage in transpersonal circles that you cannot change anything but yourself but, in changing yourself, you will find the world changes around you.' So wrote a psychologist friend, who also happens to be a practising shaman.

To effect those changes, however, we first need to know ourselves. That first step is often the most frightening because many of us don't want to face those facets of our personality or character that lurk in the shadows. By the end of this book the seeker should be ready to decide whether they wish to proceed further or, if they do not wish to confront their own personal 'demons', to abandon the quest. This is as it should be. Each of us must have the freedom to make our own decisions, based on how well we have come to know ourselves and recognise our own personal spiritual needs.

Exploring Spirituality is a voyage of discovery and, as with every journey, it is vital to find out where we are; where we think we wish to go and what methods are at our disposal for getting there. The only additional concern for those embarking on a spiritual journey is the discovery of who we are, before we can address other issues. To know yourself is to discover whether you are a walker or sprinter, a leader or a follower, a solitary worker or a team player, a mover or a shaker. To help you on your quest we recommend that you keep a personal journal as a record of your travels, thoughts, observations and discoveries as you work towards your destination. Upon arrival you will then be ready to consider implementing the changes within yourself.

Taking the First Steps

Our spiritual journey is going to start at a railway station. Imagine you are standing on the edge of a platform facing towards the platform on the opposite side of the tracks. You catch sight of yourself in the reflective glass of the waiting room window. What do you see? Does the image reflect you as you *really* are; as you see yourself; or as others see you? Maybe the reflection is distorted like that in a fairground hall of mirrors. Who exactly is that person? Why do you need to go on this journey?

Now look at the people standing on the platform opposite; what does their appearance *tell* you about them? The confident young girl, showing too much leg and cleavage for a commuter train, may be concealing behind her projected sexual allure an insecure longing for someone to show her some genuine affection. The immaculate businessman with the expensive briefcase gives an aura of calm and self-containment but how do you know he's not on his way to court to do battle with his ex-wife over custody for their children? The grey house-mouse next to him may be giving herself a day out as a treat but equally, she may be one of the hottest legal minds in marine law at Lloyds. The human race is adept at projection and concealment so it is unwise to jump to any hasty conclusions about your fellow travellers – learn that outward appearances tell you nothing.

Our outward actions often belie the inner turmoil we face when confronted with the realisation that the faith or culture in which we grew up no longer has any meaning for us. Or that we have doubts that others won't address with us. We mask the uncertainty by proclaiming that we are searching for something, while concealing the fact that we are frightened of what we might find out about life, or discover about ourselves. In reality, *all of us* are searching for something – a job, a lover, a way to mark our passage through this life, so that at the end it can be said that we 'achieved' something – something permanent to leave behind as an indication that we were here and left our mark.

Can We Take Control?

Many of us find we want more; we want to 'be' something rather than to have simply 'done' something. And then we want (or need) to understand the meaning behind all this wanting. Why life deals us the cards it does. Why we have to be born to our 'lot' and why sometimes our loved ones have to die in tragic circumstances. Is there a way around life's rules? Can we have our cake and eat it? And can we take a measure of control over some of the things that happen to us and around us?

That is when, hopefully, we realise that we are indeed spiritual beings on a very human journey, but first we need to ask ourselves some personal questions that need some honest character analysis.

Try it now	Write down answers for these questions:

Write down answers for these questions:

◆ What are your positive character traits, and what are your negative ones?

◆ Are you generally a team player or do you prefer solitary activities, and why?

◆ If you could have any three wishes, what would they be?

Closely examine what you have written for each question and look at how non-judgemental your answers have been. Correct any words that have subjective overtones.

When looking at your positive/negative traits, examine how negatives can turn into positives. For example: **anger** at exclusion caused women to fight for the vote – **anger** at needless infant deaths spurred research into cot-death syndrome, etc. Then look at how positives can become negatives when inappropriately placed or manifested – **protective** can become smothering or **easy-going** can be seen as indifferent.

There is no stigma attached to the fact that you prefer your own company but it may mean that your quest will throw up obstacles that you will have to overcome without the help of others. This way may prove harder but it may give far more personal satisfaction in the long run. Team players tend to be more gregarious, respond better to outside stimulus provided by other people but often find it difficult to function without a group sounding-board.

What did those three wishes tell you about yourself? Were you being realistic about what you wanted. Or were you wishing for something unattainable, impossible or transient? At the beginning of this chapter we opened with the words: *you cannot change anything but yourself but, in changing yourself, you will find the world changes around you.* If you implement those changes, can those wishes be fulfilled? For example, there's little point in dreaming about becoming a best-selling novelist if you've never written a word of fiction in your life. Joining a writing group could be the first step . . . *you* are the only one who can make things happen.

Why Are You Reading This Book?

Possibly because you need some help with your quest and probably because you want answers to some very pertinent questions. Such as:

◆ Where were we before we were born?
◆ Where do we go when we die?
◆ What is the meaning of life?
◆ What is the purpose of living?

These are the usual questions *behind* the questions that people ask concerning their own search for spirituality. This line of questioning is often expressed by the seeker in the form of: 'I want something to believe in', or 'I want a direction to my life', and occasionally, 'I want to connect with something that I can believe to be true'.

Learning to explore our own spirituality enables ordinary people to find their own answers to many of these questions. It teaches us how to recognise that truth is subjective, according to where the individual is standing *at the precise moment at which they pose the question* – and very often based on some previous personal experience. What appears as inspiration to one, however, will be completely incomprehensible to another.

> Like fingerprints, spiritual truth is unique to the individual seeker, since there are no pre-set rules to govern how and where it is to be found.

Do you reject this apparent lack of cohesion as unacceptable? If you do, you don't stand alone, because in our quick-fix, sound-bite society there are many who believe it is their 'right' to be *given* the truth. Are you one of those who demand to be shown direction; to be instructed in how to interpret a belief, or coached through a course in order to pass on to a higher level? Some people even want to be told which religion, philosophy or path is right for them. They need to have their world-view confirmed that X is right and Y is wrong; that the new they are seeking is better than the old they wish to abandon.

Try it now   Here you need to consider three points and record your reaction in your journal:

- ◆ What do you do when faced with two or more conflicting truths?
- ◆ Do you seek to avoid problems or overcome them?
- ◆ Do you accumulate information and the benefit of other people's experience in preparation for a possible need, or do you wait for a circumstance to occur before acquiring the relevant information?

Truth is 40 Shades of Grey

There are few things in this life that can be categorised into simple terms of black and white – the genuine seeker on a spiritual quest will eventually come to see the world in 40 shades of grey. This does not mean indecision or developing an eclectic frame of mind: in a spiritual context this often means that there is certainly more than one way of arriving at the truth. More often than not, the proselytising faiths condemn other religions as being misguided, or even evil, yet by what right does one denounce another for his perceived error of judgement in worship? Is it so difficult to understand that *both* could be right, that every religion is merely a means of 'coming to God' by a different path?

Ignoring problems never manages to solve them. Pushing a problem away often compounds the difficulties and by the time direct action is unavoidable, the original problem has been magnified out of all proportion. Facing up to a difficulty doesn't solve it, but awareness that it exists does sometimes offer up a solution when you are least expecting it. Changing spiritual direction may solve a problem or create new ones, so how are you going to cope?

In his book *Ancient Wisdom, Modern World*, His Holiness the Dalai Lama calls for a spiritual revolution on a global scale by harnessing the 'universal principles we can draw on which transcend the dilemma of belief or unbelief'. He has no desire for the global population to become Buddhist; he would much rather people of other faiths developed a greater understanding and acceptance of Buddhism, whilst remaining firmly within their own religion. The wider we delve into the intricacies of other beliefs, the more we come to realise just how similar we all are when it boils down to the basic fundamentals of faith.

Where Did It Go Wrong?

Experience has shown that many people, when asked about their previous religious experiences, will say that they have tried it and didn't like it – time to 'move on to something different' rather than 'gone as far as I can at the moment and need a fresh way of re-connecting with it.' When questioned further as to whether the seeker has looked for further instruction from their own priesthood, the response is usually negative and somewhat derogatory towards that particular religion as a whole.

These responses suggest that some see their religious activity as a form of insurance. Perhaps they see it as obtaining approval or certification for being good; some kind of passport to heaven. 'If I do this, nothing bad will happen.' But what happens when something *does* go wrong? There is usually a sense of outrage or betrayal. This mainly because the person concerned feels that they've played by the rules and been dumped on by God, who obviously ignored the fact that they've observed all the necessary religious rites and festivals and have been seen to be doing so by the rest of the congregation.

In other cases the quarrel is with the priesthood and its dogma rather than the religion itself. In this instance there is no quarrel with 'God' but with his intermediary. There is often the accusation that the priesthood has lost the plot by injecting new methods of worship into the established ritual; or the unsympathetic handling of a family/personal rite of passage. Couple this with a real or imagined alienation caused by misunderstandings of theological jargon and we are faced with what we consider to be a 'wounded soul' – wounded by disappointment, bereavement, a perceived betrayal or disillusionment.

The Knee-Jerk Reaction

At this stage it is often perceived as being a logical step to explore or convert to another faith, thereby embracing what is seen as a different set of values or an alternative morality. These knee-jerk explorations can lure the seeker into dangerous waters simply because many people insist on confusing religion with spirituality. The 'smells and bells', in addition to all the other unfamiliar trappings of a different set of rituals, can, through the allure of 'strangeness', have the most awe-inspiring effect on a newcomer to the fold.

Try it now   Try to be objective about the reasons why you need a new
direction.

+ Have you come from a family faith or cultural background
  that you now feel has become stifling?
+ Has the priesthood changed the rules and you feel unhappy
  with the innovations?
+ Conversely, have you had an upbringing in which religion
  played a minor, or non-existent role, and now feel that you've
  missed out on something indefinable?

Remember: whatever the reasons for bringing about this change it
is bound to cause upset and/or confusion within the family or
cultural group. Expect to be confronted by anger or hurt from
your priest and family, and last but not least, total bewilderment
from your friends who wonder what undisclosed crisis has caused
you to go out and get religion!

Satisfying a Spiritual Hunger

Dissatisfaction with the family faith can arise for a variety of
reasons. As the different ethnic groups merge together in the
classroom, the cultural barriers are slowly being eroded. Hindu
girls falls in love with Christian boys, Muslim teenagers refuse to
bow to the traditional arranged marriages and Jewish friends
share a bacon sandwich with Gentile colleagues.

Many parents who follow a dogmatic faith experience heartache
when their children test their spirituality against the religion and
'rebel'. Depending on whether this is seen and dealt with as
exploration or total rejection, it can be enhancing and lead to a
fuller understanding of the family faith – or a point of irreparable
damage and loss.

Try as they might, many parents who insist on maintaining the
rigid disciplines of their fundamentalist faith often experience the
pain of a son or daughter apparently breaking away from their
roots.

Once the fear of divine wrath has been removed, however, it's
but a small step to go looking at other religions and cultures but,

more often than not, these new seekers don't *really* know what they are looking for. The 'spiritual tourists' – those who've been 'into' Buddhism, Wicca and Druidry and Asatru and Shinto (often originally from a Christian background) and still not found what they are looking for – are probably the least discerning folk. They remind you of someone who visits the restaurants of the world's finest cuisine and haven't the sense to open the menu to page two, so all they've ever managed to order and taste is the soup. Then they wonder why their appetites are never sated and they still have a craving for solid food.

Why do they do that?

Exploring and studying the different religious paths without commitment is a good place to start since it encourages thought and consideration when you can say: 'That's interesting, why do they do that?' Go to your local library and choose a selection of books on the world's religions (see Further Reading for suggestions). This simple exercise may not give you the answers you're looking for but it will satisfy the craving for information, if not the direction, and may show just how little you know about other people's religious beliefs. Ask yourself:

◆ Apart from your own, which other religion do you know the most about?
◆ Do you have any close, personal friends from a different faith?
◆ Do you know how to behave in a church, mosque, temple or synagogue?

Don't worry – *few* people know how to behave outside their own religion but this is a good time to start because the more you understand about religious differences, the easier it will be to spot the similarities between them.

Responsibility Towards Self

'Religion is for those people who are scared of going to hell, and spirituality is for those of us who have been there!' I don't recall where I heard that, or who said it, but it's stuck in my mind and made me think about how I would define the two words. Spirituality, by my definition, is a state of 'being' and religion is that of 'doing'.

The nature of her work as a residential care manager means that some of Liz's elderly residents depart this life whilst in her care. This makes her very conscious of her own responsibility about other people's views and beliefs, while not making a great outward show of her own deeply held convictions.

'My spirituality is the part of me that knows I have a place within the universe and a relationship with all it contains,' says Liz. 'In a way it is a work in progress – the more I seek, the more I find. It is ever growing, ever changing, reshaping and redefining *me*. Religion is the means by which I express, celebrate and honour my spirituality.'

There is a problem with trying to reconcile these two words, religion and spirituality, because we are looking at things that are deeply personal and form part of our very state of existence. They are at the heart of our very selves even if we deny the existence of spirituality and question the validity of religion. Any definition is, therefore, going to be subjective, which is why I began with a quote from someone else. It was a valid definition for them, although I suspect that many people would argue with it.

Because Liz works in one of the caring professions within a local authority it is necessary for her to have a healthy respect and a wide understanding of the different beliefs of the people in her charge – even though they may in practice or dogma differ from her own. Nearer to home, however, it is well to remember that none of us lives in a vacuum and that our behaviour affects others, both directly and indirectly. Whilst we have every responsibility to ourselves to explore the spiritual path of our own choosing, this does not mean we should ride rough-shod over the feelings of our nearest and dearest.

Try it now	Take a moment to reflect on the *long-term* repercussions of your actions.

- Would a change or deepening of faith cause a major family row?
- Is there a particular member of the family (of whom you are particularly fond) who would be deeply offended by your change of path?
- Do you have the courage and strength to cope with a family rift?

At this point in our quest it isn't necessary to have all the answers to these questions but it's a good time to reflect on the changes we could bring about in the lives of others. Going to the other extreme is the story of the heroin addict who converted to a fundamentalist version of Christianity. The family were overjoyed by his rejection of drugs but the price *they* have to pay is 'enduring his relentless efforts to convert them from their mild attachment to Christianity to his newly discovered full-frontal fundamentalism.'

Be Realistic in Following Your Quest

When we begin to examine the different religions and philosophies we should be looking for what is beyond and deeper than the level at which we are currently thinking. This involves junking all prejudices and talking with those who obviously live their spirituality, and finding out how they apply their way of life, their knowledge. Take the opportunity to explore, think, debate and discuss but do not make any commitment (or judgements) until you are sure of your goal, no matter how tempting the promises of a charismatic guru.

Should you feel that this is some form of faith-less liberalism, or convenient spiritual gymnastics, here we will include the views of two eminent theologians from opposite sides of the world but with a single thought: that one does not need religion to follow a moral and ethical spiritual path. Both men are aware of the problems that arise from confusing 'ritual pieties' with morality.

Richard Holloway, Bishop of Edinburgh and Gresham Professor of Divinity in the City of London, often finds himself in hot water because of his views. 'Many religious leaders say that without a belief in God and in absolute standards there can be no genuine moral conduct; that the moral confusions of our own time are directly related to the erosion of religion in Western society . . . Genuinely good things can be in conflict with one another, so that mature people try to learn to live with contradictions rather than insisting on neat resolutions . . . Our search for basic moral principles, if we are wise, will always allow for situational variations.'

As the Bishop points out, morality attempts to base itself on observed consequences, not on beliefs, superstitions or preferences. For instance while many of us do not believe it is wrong to eat pork or drink alcohol, in the presence of a Muslim moral courtesy should oblige us to abstain. Similarly we should take the trouble to remove our shoes on entering a mosque and cover our heads when visiting a synagogue.

HH the Dalai Lama warns that we should accept 'that many who reject religion do so out of convictions sincerely held, not merely because they are unconcerned with the deeper questions of human existence.' We would be extremely unwise to assume that such people are lacking a sense of right and wrong or of what is morally appropriate just because some anti-religionists are immoral. Religious belief is no guarantee of moral integrity.

Using religion to re-connect

Here we must acknowledge the fact that although the majority of the planet's six billion human beings may claim allegiance to one faith or another, the influence of religion on people's lives is, generally speaking, marginal. 'It is doubtful whether, globally, even a billion are what I would call dedicated religious practitioners: people who try, on a daily basis, faithfully to follow the principles and precepts of their faith,' concluded His Holiness. Those who *are* dedicated practitioners follow a diverse number of religious traditions because no single religion satisfies all of humanity. By contrast, the rest of humanity falls into the category of 'non-practising' that shows we *can* live quite well without any commitment to religion.

There are a lot of religions out there – some ancient, some relatively new. The word religion means to 're-connect' and each religion is the method by which its members seek to re-connect with their souls and answer some of those questions we all ask about our mortality and beyond. The religions themselves are not the answer, but a means by which an answer might be found – and you might just find it hidden in the one you're about to abandon.

Case Study

When Barry was 8, his father abandoned the family, and as an antidote to her depression and feeling of failure his mother turned to the Mormon Church for solace. Although both parents were teachers, Barry the was victim of a learning disability that made him a poor scholar. As a result he was made to feel like an abject failure both at school and within the Church, which drove him to attempt suicide when he was 16 years of age.

Instead of attempting to get to the root of the problem, the boy was lectured by Church elders about the sin he'd committed against God by trying to kill himself. As a consequence for the next 20 years Barry pursued every anti-social pathway that would be diametrically opposed to the teachings of the Mormon Church. He also went out of his way to offend his mother's religious sensibilities, which he blamed for his inability to make relationships on any level.

Although he progressed no further than sensational books and videos, by the time he was 37 years old he had developed an extremely unbalanced leaning towards satanism and anything that *he* could identify as 'black magic', whether it was fact or fiction. He had cultivated a negative attitude to everything that he saw as social values or responsibility. He openly bragged about being a black magician and a disciple of Aleister Crowley, which didn't endear him to his psychologist or anyone else either.

Despite his learning disability Barry was a highly intelligent person. The first hurdle to be overcome was his rejection of any positive suggestion which brought about his response: 'You're just like the Mormons!' and a slamming down of his phone. The second was to introduce him to a mentor who did not blanch at his outrageous and often offensive 'black magician persona' and who was at least *au fait* with occult terminology.

Barry refused point-blank to return to any form of discussion on Mormon doctrine which he considered the instrument of ruin in his life. In little over a year he was introduced to a set of very different spiritual avenues and instructed on the use of the Christian Qabalah at a very simple level. Barry wasn't *really* interested in black magic and occultism but it was the only thing he'd found that could induce apoplexy in the Church Elders and upset his mother. He merely wanted to be different and to be noticed. Gradually his anger and bitterness subsided as his mentor encouraged him to discard the satanic symbolism and develop a more positive attitude towards himself and his relationship with his mother.

Here we have an example of someone with a self-perceived need to rebel purely for the sake of giving offence, going against established teaching and as an attention-seeking device. The allure of occultism was guaranteed to get the Church Elders hopping mad and he enjoyed the effect it caused. There was, however, no *real* desire to explore genuine esoteric teaching because he was consciously afraid of the 'satanic' elements he'd read about in the Dennis Wheatley books. The Christian Qabalah provided an alternative vehicle for his devotions in a familiar Biblical setting, although it is doubtful whether he will ever return to the Mormon Church. _____

Summary

The points raised in this chapter will have made you think about the differences between your religion and your own personal spiritual goals in a much more positive way. Consider the following:

- ◆ What do you feel is lacking in your present situation which is stifling your spiritual growth?
- ◆ Has familiarity bred contempt or indifference?
- ◆ Would a different approach allow you to re-connect with your faith?

Ultimately religion should help us find our sense of spirituality, and allow us the freedom to express ourselves within a recognisable framework, but it should not bind us with dogma. Nor should there be rules to state what is or is not a religious belief, whether it be public or private.

Liberalism
isn't always
the answer to
the needs of
the many.

CHAPTER 2

Healing the Wounded Soul

Just as we alone can implement changes within ourselves, very often we alone are the instruments of our own unhappiness, albeit sometimes unwittingly. We can wound ourselves spiritually by taking umbrage when we believe that our God has ratted on the agreement, i.e. we feel let down when something happens which we think God (or our belief in God) should have prevented. We reach a crisis of faith exacerbated by disappointment, bereavement or disillusionment that often results in our turning our back on church or temple and seeking an alternative.

Many a bemused cleric has been held responsible for God's shortcomings when he's totally oblivious of the cause of so much anger. On the other side of the coin are the time-honoured clichés about 'the will of God' and the tenets of the faith, which some members of the priesthood resort to because they have no other weapons in their armoury with which to relieve the anguish of an injured party. We have, of course, returned to the condition of the 'wounded soul' and the misunderstanding of theological jargon.

But it's not just the major religions where it can all go wrong. Break-away fringe groups, cults and alternative faiths have all caused their fair share of disappointment when a convert suddenly wakes up one enlightened morning and realises they've made a *big* mistake. Unfortunately, in some cases leaving isn't as easy as joining – with disastrous results for both the individual involved and the families who have been living through the nightmare. In this case we find the soul doubly wounded because the 'betrayal' has been compounded by yet another rejection.

Living with the Pain of Loss

Liz, who is both a spiritual mentor and residential care manager, maintains that *everyone* is a wounded soul, carrying the scars of our existence throughout our lives: 'We can be damaged in various ways, sometimes through our own ignorance, carelessness or spiritual high jinx (go on, admit it, we've all done that).' All too often the wounding occurs at the hands of another, sometimes without meaning to, sometimes through exploitation or manipulation and is associated with the loss of something important.

'What I find deeply worrying is if the person responsible for the wounding is in a position of sacred trust – parents, teachers and priests', Liz continues. 'Most worrying of all is if that person *is* a member of the priesthood of any path: priesthood is priesthood whether we talk about Christian, Jew, Hindu, Moslem or Pagan. I can only speak from first-hand knowledge of two of these, but it seems awfully easy for anyone to enter the lay-ministry these days. There are unqualified people setting up churches, temples and groups all the time with no form of registration or control but they attract the gullible with their promises of instant enlightenment. When will people learn there is no shortcut, everything takes time – rush it and you can start counting those wounded souls.'

Causes of spiritual loss

This 'loss' can evolve from different root causes. For example, official figures from a Christian Research Survey show that the number of regular worshippers is plummeting; particularly in the case of 'trendy vicars and their nonsensical sermons', who are losing more ground than the traditional churches. The traditionalists do not welcome a clergy who are more akin to patronising social workers. With the spread of this new approach to God, many are turning away from the local church when a new incumbent turns out to be more 'progressive' than a dearly loved and respected former vicar. In other words, people are not necessarily losing their faith or spiritual identity – *it is being taken away from them.*

This has been confirmed by a report by Professor Peter Colman of the University of Southampton, based on a 20-year study that shows that people lose faith as they grow older and feel more isolated from their church. In 1977, 64 per cent of the pensioners taking part in the survey regarded themselves as members of the Church of England. Of these, a third attended religious services,

88 per cent listened to religious broadcasts and 70 per cent said that religion meant much to them. By 1998, 37 per cent said religion meant less than it had when they were younger; only 47 per cent said it was important to them. Professor Coleman said that this did not necessarily mean that they had lost their belief, but that they had stopped feeling that they were church members, confounding the idea that they become more religious as they approach death. 'The loss of social, psychological and spiritual support from churches may mean that older people with spiritual needs are more vulnerable,' he concluded.

There has also been a good deal of criticism from traditionalist Catholics that too many Masses in Catholic churches are now considered to be uninspiring and dull. As a recent communication in *The Daily Telegraph* pointed out, however, the fault lies not with the modern Mass but with the 'laziness and ineptitude of priests and choirmasters'. According to the writer, the 1970 Missal of Paul IV 'permits all the things they want: Latin; beautiful music, clouds of incense and even an eastward-facing celebration' and that it is up to the congregation to encourage priests to use the new Mass properly. This means dialogue must be entered into and discussions conducted in a sensible and thought-provoking manner.

Surprisingly enough, spiritual loss can also manifest in those who have had little or no religious instruction. RI as it was called (religious instruction) was eased out of the school curriculum in the late 1960s as a result of parental pressure and the growing number of children with different ethnic backgrounds. Thirty years later, when *The Sunday Times* conducted a special poll of 18-years olds – the so-called Y2K Generation – it showed that a staggering 77 per cent of those interviewed had no religious beliefs at all, nor any interest in religion or spirituality. Many of these young people *will* eventually seek 'something' to fill the void and, human nature being what it is, they will probably turn to the assortment of eclectic New Age beliefs since here there is generally little demand for commitment.

Try it now Do you feel that your present spiritual confusion results from:
- ◆ Unfulfilling religious instruction?
- ◆ A difference of opinion with a member of the priesthood?

◆ Doubt in the existence of God according to the teaching of your own faith?

If you've answered 'yes' to any of the above, it may be that your quest needs to follow a period of solitary exploration of different faiths in order to re-establish what it is that you're looking for. This does not involve 'giving up' on your own religion; it is merely a way of broadening your outlook by examining things from a different perspective. Use the resources at your local library and don't be afraid to take out children's books on the religions of the world. Obviously they tend to over simplify things but they do cut through the waffle found in so many books written for adults.

'My Priest Doesn't Understand Me!'

In this instance we often find the reason behind the antagonism is the refusal of the priest to condone certain behaviour in which we want to participate, but which goes against the teaching of that particular religious establishment. Nevertheless, liberalism isn't always the answer when it comes to providing for the needs of the many over those of the individual, especially when it refers to moral or social issues which are the mainstay of that faith or tradition:

◆ In these enlightened times of free speech and political correctness, many people believe they have the right to flout the rules without censorship and yet still remain part of a formal religious grouping. For example, the Roman Catholic Church's stance on birth control may be considered archaic and impractical in many quarters but a 'loyal' Roman Catholic is duty bound to accept the directive without question. Here we cannot 'maintain the right to propagate opinions contrary to the teaching authority of the Church' whilst demanding the right to be classed as a loyal member of that establishment. One is either a 'Roman' Catholic or a dissident catholic and those bending the rules on birth control are, in fact, *dissidents.*

◆ Similarly, because of the liberal appearances of Buddhism in Western eyes, the Dalai Lama is often petitioned to publicly condone homosexuality but as he explained recently in an interview: 'I am a Buddhist and for a Buddhist, a relationship between two men is wrong. If two men really love each other and are not religious, then that is okay by me.' Here we find no moral judgement but the message *is* loud and clear: homosexuality has no place within the tenets of the true Buddhist faith. In fact, on the subject of abortion, homosexuality and marriage, the Dalai Lama's position differs little from that of the Pope.

♦ Within orthodox Judaism it is not uncommon for the family to observe *shiveh* (a seven-day, traditional mourning period) if a daughter marries out of the faith. Again, on the surface this appears barbaric in the twenty-first century but a person's 'Jewishness' is determined through the blood-line of the mother, not inclination, and the religious laws still guard against the defilement of racial purity.

♦ Sometimes a priest decides to take a personal moral stance, as in a recent case of a rector refusing to baptise children of unmarried couples because they are 'living in sin'. A spokesman said that while every child living within a Church of England parish has the basic right to be baptised, parochial church councils could decide their own policies. Although it is unusual for a priest to refuse to baptise a child, the vicar had the final say on the grounds that he was acting in accordance with church and Bible teaching.

♦ Rejection can come not from the priesthood but from the church members. Following the christening of the surrogate twins fathered by a gay couple, the baptism (unique in church history) was criticised by parishioners who said it was 'morally wrong'. The vicar defended his decision to carry out the service: 'The Church does not make any distinction about parents. We baptise the children of single parents and couples who are cohabiting. It is not for other people to penalise any child or shut them out.'

Situations such as these can lead to a rejection of the priesthood and religion rather than a belief in God. Here the external trappings of the priesthood are seen but not the actual person wearing the cloth. Those wearing it are perceived as being different; as having to maintain a different (or unsympathetic) code of conduct – or even being seen to be no better than they are. The whole notion of 'them versus us' comes into play rather than accepting that those of the priesthood are on their own spiritual journey, often being just as fallible, questioning and human as those who are rejecting them.

The priesthood is also perceived as being in possession of the answers, because they are priests and therefore initiated into the 'secrets' of their particular religion, instead of having taken the step of total commitment to that religion. They are often still learning how to manifest their inner spirituality in the outside world. This mental (and frequently vitriolic) separation between laity and priesthood of any religion may be a recurring theme throughout the seeker's quest for truth.

The Ego-Centric Society

These attitudes reflect the changes from a socio-centric to an ego-centric society, whereby the religious focus (church, temple, etc.) is seen not as a gathering point for a community, but as a convenient pseudo-spiritual watering-hole for the individual.

> The cult of the individual now demands that the orthodox religion is tailored to meet the requirements of the consumer age and, as a result, folk only want to be bothered with religion when it suits them.

When the church, for example, can provide a pretty back-drop for a costly family wedding, christening or funeral, the vicar is expected to welcome everyone with open arms without regular attendance being part of the package.

Whether we like it or not, most people live life by the creed of: what's in it for me? But if we have spiritual needs that go unmet it is *not unreasonable* for us to go out and seek an alternative that offers a more intellectually stimulating approach. At this stage it does not mean that we need to find an alternative religion, just a different perspective. In our grandparent's day it would still have caused social disapproval to step outside our own religious community, even if the family weren't staunch worshippers. In our parent's day it was almost unheard of for those of different cultures to mix socially and even today, in our multicultural society, how many children sleep over in the homes of school-friends of a different race or religion?

If we are forced to live in an ego-centric society, we should at least turn it to our own spiritual advantage by encouraging dialogue with those whose life-style and religion are different. When we take away the cultural trappings and ways of speaking we will discover a rich vein of experience, just waiting to be tapped – regardless of our individual backgrounds.

Try it now   Record your own personal attitudes to *organised* religion.
- ◆ Do you feel that the religion should serve the needs of the people?
- ◆ Should people be encouraged to worship how, where and when they choose?
- ◆ Should cross-cultural religious education be compulsory in schools?

Again the key question is whether you wish to follow your quest as part of some organised grouping, or whether you want to go it alone and discover how other people travel on their spiritual journey.

'I'd Believe in God if Only He'd . . .'

Quite a few people look upon their dealings with their God as some sort of bargain basement where they can pick up the odd remnant without having to pay through the nose for it. Others demand some kind of miraculous cabaret trick to 'prove' the existence of the Divine, never stopping to think that God might actually object to being treated like a second-rate conjuror.

This cavalier treatment, or even questioning the existence of God, is not a new phenomenon. As A. M. Wilson observed in his book *God's Funeral*, 'No sooner have the intelligentsia confined the Almighty to the history books than popular opinion rises against them.' Nevertheless questions such as 'If God is omnipotent, can he create a rock that even he can't lift?' is constantly used to challenge the existence of a supreme deity that is all things to all of humankind.

'Prove it!' syndrome seems to strike at the heart of most of today's spiritual seeking, especially by those who profess to have, (a) no religious belief, or (b) a violent opposition to the orthodox religions. The poor old Creator *can't* be all things to all men and women. He, She or It will always stub a toe on someone's prejudices and so the 'proof' that the sceptic demands will remain out of reach. The proof will eventually manifest in the eyes of the genuine seeker but it won't be the same for you as it was for the authors of this book; neither will your experience match the sensations felt by other readers.

Try it now	Try to define your personal image of God and how you see Him/Her/It in the grand scheme of things. Is the image of:

- A benign, patriarchal/matriarchal figure?
- Being 'out there' or conversely 'in me'?
- A divine creative force?

For the majority of people around the world it is necessary to have an image of God cast in their own likeness, i.e. human form, in order to relate to Him/Her. On the other hand Celts, Sikhs, Muslims and Jews worship their deity in a more abstract form; in some cases not even speaking the name of God. The religious art from around the world makes a fascinating study and tells us more in terms of artistic representation than words can ever convey about how the people from other cultures see their God(s).

Inability to Cope with Another's Sufferings

Compassion for our fellows is the cornerstone of the majority of religions and few can go through life without being affected in some way by the sufferings of others. The Buddhist canon is full of exhortations to have compassion for other people in order to elevate the soul to new heights of spirituality and attain happiness. In reality, most people find the suffering of others a bit of an embarrassment on several counts. Physical manifestation of disfigurement or illness often results in a shying away from the afflicted because of embarrassment to be seen in their company in case it's catching! Mental or emotional problems can cause embarrassment because people often do not know what to do or say to help. Social difficulties, such as divorce or scandal, can result in embarrassment of association.

Developing compassion

We also find it almost impossible to feel compassion for others if we not feeling good about ourselves. Suffering from low self-esteem isn't conducive to developing a compassionate and tolerant approach to daily living, never mind finding the balance of complete mental and spiritual freedom. Nevertheless the development of compassion is more than being kindly disposed towards others – human or animal – it is an integral part of spiritual growth. In Buddhist terms it can be defined as *non-violent, non-harming and non-aggressive* - a mental attitude with:

◆ A sense of commitment, responsibility and respect towards others (human and animal).

◆ A sense of affinity and closeness with others (human and animal).

◆ A state of mind that wishes these things for yourself.

Psychiatrist Howard Cutler observes that recent studies confirm that developing compassion and altruism has a positive impact on our physical and emotional health. Not only that, but interacting with others in a warm and compassionate way dramatically increases life expectancy, while a positive state of mind can improve physical health. It stands to reason that if improved health and self-esteem can be gained by feeling *genuine* compassion for another's suffering, then this is also the beginning for healing a wounded soul.

Try it now

Be honest – how do you *currently* rate in the compassion stakes?

◆ How would you describe your level of compassion: high, low or average?

◆ Do you feel more compassion for animals than humans?

◆ Do you currently engage in *any* form of voluntary work?

In all fairness it *is* extremely difficult to feel any degree of compassion for those in unfortunate circumstances these days. This is largely due to intensive media coverage that has caused us to become immune to the shocking images appearing repeatedly on our television screens and magazines. The eye can no longer differentiate between fact and fiction and, as a result, the brain no longer registers that the disaster is happening to *real* people. Look at what's going on nearer to home and remember that a small, heart-felt expenditure of effort can be as world-changing as the grand gesture.

The Pain of Disappointment

Before we can experience genuine feelings of compassion for others, however, we need to put our own house in order. To do this we must understand the root of our own pain or sense of loss/disappointment.

Disappointment comes from not achieving or gaining something we'd set our mind on. For example, a bright student taking a study course at college would be disappointed at only gaining a B grade; a student who was less capable would be delighted with a B because they didn't expect to pass. The former might anticipate rejection from potential employers for not achieving top marks; the latter would seek out a better position because the pass marks were higher than expected.

A sense of disappointment is, therefore, relative to the individual and situation. In spiritual terms this can apply to the expectations we have, or what we strive for in accordance with our social or family background. In *Intelligent Emotion*, psychotherapist Frances Wilks maintains that many of life's disappointments come about because we focus on the outcome of an experience rather than the process of getting there. 'We demand that the experience yield us what we want rather than allow it to simply *be.*'

We may join a group or organisation that promises to teach one of the many spiritual development techniques but after a certain period of time we have experienced nothing out of the ordinary. This feeling of failure is compounded because the others in the group appear only too willing to discuss their own results at length. *We* joined because we wanted to reach out and grasp that indefinable something – but despite our efforts we never achieved that blinding flash of inspiration.

This is because our efforts have been concentrated on the flash itself, not on the process of building up to receive it. Because we decide in advance what we want or expect from a situation, we then demand that the results be provided along the lines of our own individual fantasy. 'We construct all sorts of fantasies and then feel very frustrated when they don't come about,' concluded Frances Wilks. As a result we dismiss the instruction as a waste of time and, although we are the ones who are doing the rejecting, there is still an element of failure lurking under the surface.

◆ **Physical/mental**: A feeling of intense frustration.
◆ **Emotional/psychological**: Our self-confidence and self-esteem suffers.
◆ **Spiritual**: The fantasy was unable to compare favourably with reality.

Result

Rejection of ideas on a mundane level which, if they are not consciously dealt with, may grow out of all proportion. We view the situation as being *our* choice to walk away, which masks our disappointment at *them* not wanting us there because our efforts weren't good enough. Even if we are the ones rejecting, it may stem from a feeling (real or imagined) of personal rejection by the group; the power to walk away may *appear* to be in our hands when, in fact, it is not.

The Pain of Bereavement

The loss of someone close to us can have far-reaching and devastating effects. Conversely it can also draw on unsuspected inner strengths. When bereavement causes us to question our faith or belief in our God, it may take a considerable amount of time (if ever) for us to accept the death of a loved one, particularly in the case of a sudden heart attack, an unexpected death through accident, or the loss of a child.

The pain remains for several reasons:
◆ there wasn't the chance to say goodbye
◆ the manner of the death
◆ things were left unsaid
◆ remorse over being the one to remain alive
◆ not having done enough while the deceased was still living
◆ the living and the dead parted company on bad terms.

Even the Dalai Lama, in an interview with Howard Cutler, confessed that in addition to the sadness he experienced on the death of his brother, he had a lingering sense of regret. 'I was gone at the time he died, and I think if I had been there, maybe there was something I could have done to help. So I have this feeling of regret.' If one of the most respected of religious teachers can admit to such feelings, then those of us who have a lesser understanding of such matters can take comfort in knowing that a person as spiritually elevated can also suffer pangs of regret for things left undone.

While grief is a natural reaction to bereavement, it is an emotion which 'requires the application of profound imagination to resolve,' writes Frances Wilks. 'In order to come to terms with this loss, we mourn them until we're ready to let them go. Grief is a doorway from one state to another and is essential for change and development.' Nevertheless we find that no other area of the human condition can bring about such devastating reactions as bereavement and its overwhelming sense of loss:

♦ **Physical**: The physical ache of knowing that a person will never be part of our lives again; that we can never talk to them again, or explain our actions.

♦ **Mental**: The stress of coping with bereavement; its aftermath and the if-onlys.

♦ **Emotional**: An overwhelming sense of loneliness/emptiness, often coupled with guilt.

♦ **Psychological**: The death of a close relative or friend can have life-long repercussions, especially if any natural feeling of guilt is allowed to take control.

♦ **Spiritual**: A rejection of religion or spiritual belief as a result of denial and/or fear.

Result

Guilt for all the things we should (or shouldn't) have done and said. The priest/religion can become the scapegoat for all the pain of loss and the guilt that goes with it. We can also feel that God has rejected our plea for a reprieve: a miracle.

The Pain of Disillusionment

Disillusionment, in its own way, is a form of betrayal because we may have been misled into believing something to be true. Frances Wilks describes the overwhelming feeling that the world has been shattered and that everything around us appears to take on an unpleasant and distressing hue; an all-enveloping sensation that an irreplaceable something has been lost and life will never be the same again.

Spiritual disillusionment often occurs when the rug is pulled out from under our feet by a traumatic occurrence. A common scenario is the instance where a loved one is unexpectedly struck down by a fatal or debilitating illness. The profound shock and disbelief when death occurs can overshadow the grieving process, especially in a staunchly religious household, because of its previously unshakeable belief that prayer will be answered. Death is seen not as a tragic but natural rite of passage, but as a personal rejection by God and in its wake prayer is replaced by a liturgy of:

- How could God do this to me?
- Why shouldn't I hate God for doing this to me?
- Why shouldn't I hate the priest for lying to me?
- What will become of me?
- Where do I turn now?
- Is there anything left to believe in?

Should these questions remain unresolved, the wounded soul loses its grip on reality and descends into a pit of spiritual self-destruction. The disillusionment 'proves' that there is no God out there and, as the priest is seen as an instrument of the deception, s/he is denied the opportunity to offer any form of comfort or counselling. The wounded soul is left to cope alone with its problems.

- **Physical/mental**: Although the physical effects are bad enough, the mental pain is usually worse.
- **Emotional**: A source of succour and support has been removed/destroyed.
- **Psychological**: Self-confidence and self-esteem suffer because of the perceived rejection.
- **Spiritual**: Nothing remains but a bottomless pit of despair.

Result

A complete rejection and betrayal of faith by both deity and priesthood which in turn can produce a sense of fear, hatred and utter loss.

The Pain of Manipulation

The pain of manipulation can often be the greater because it compounds elements of disappointment, bereavement (in an abstract sense) and disillusionment with an overwhelming sense of betrayal. Our spirituality is our sense of 'wholeness' and an assault on any part of our person can do damage on many levels. Here we have given examples of the harm that can be done to someone when they are unprepared and poorly equipped to cope with unexpected situations of a manipulative nature.

◆ **Physical**: Being put in danger. Injury causing changes to the body.

◆ **Mental**: Sensory damage/deprivation or change. Exploitation of experiences and thoughts, manipulation of information.

◆ **Emotional/psychological**: Emotional dependence or blackmail. Manipulation of feelings such as guilt or fear.

◆ **Sexual**: Misuse of sexual power. Exploitation of sexual attraction.

◆ **Spiritual**: Irresponsible use of ritual and its energies.

Any or all of the above can be mirrored in a dozen different social or religious situations but look at the following scenario. Attractive female joins break-away religious group. Charismatic priest offers to instruct her, but naturally this involves 'giving herself' totally in ritual and physical form (possibly with onlookers). Female voices her doubts and fears but is told that this is the way of the group, otherwise she would not be fully committed; would not be able to remain with the group and would not be worthy of the priest's attentions. Female reluctantly agrees and goes through with the induction.

Before spluttering and saying 'Oh yeah!', consider the hunger you are experiencing in the pursuit of knowledge and spiritual fulfilment, and what you might have done to satisfy it. Now look at the six categories again from a wider perspective and perhaps you'll have a better understanding of the damage that can be done.

◆ **Physically**: The act itself took place (sometimes publicly) with someone the woman would not ordinarily have taken as a lover. She did not know the sexual history of the priest and sex was quite probably unprotected which can be dangerous.

- ◆ **Mental/psychological**: The priest was playing on the woman's lack of knowledge of the 'religion' and its practices. He is manipulating information to suit his purpose.
- ◆ **Emotional**: 'If you don't do this you can't be a member of the group and you'll be out in the cold.' Rejection by the group and the priest is felt as tantamount to rejection by God. This is manipulating her fears and needs; she goes through with the act because she needs to follow her path and is left to pay the price.
- ◆ **Sexual**: Sirens blaring and alarms screaming on this one. Not only has the woman been raped sexually (and rape is *not* too strong a word here); her sexuality and sexual energy have been abused. She may have said 'yes' because it was that or lose everything she'd come to believe in; saying 'no' was not an option.
- ◆ **Spiritual**: Misuse of ritual for the priest's own gratification of sexual need and exhibitionism.

Result

Total betrayal of trust and wounds that will take years (forever?) to heal. Fear, hatred (of self and others, particularly males), guilt and loss. Substitute the word teacher or parent for priest and you can formulate your own scenario. And the victims aren't necessarily women; men can also be manipulated by the same powerful quest for spiritual fulfilment.

Spiritual Depression

Mel is a member of the priesthood and has heard many of these stories in her role as a spiritual mentor. 'In the case of manipulation, it would be so convenient and easy to dismiss claims such as this as proof of satanic practice, but in reality the majority that come to light are those perpetuated by break-away cults whose doctrines are based on *Christian* writ. The leaders of any group which practises sexual initiation are usually power-freaks and well versed in the psychology of guilt and shame, which means that no one is going to make any complaints to the police.

'Rape by psychological coercion might not appear the same as being attacked in a dark alley by an unknown assailant, but it is equally damaging. This is a double betrayal because the victim may have looked upon them as a friend *and* a priest. The only way to deal with this kind of suggestion is to laugh in the priest's face and tell him (or her) to take a hike. There isn't a *genuine* spiritual or religious path on this earth that demands sexual initiation at beginner's level, no matter what you've been told – and that includes any of the pagan-based faiths, too.'

> Guilt and rejection are the two main causes of spiritual depression just as they are root causes for many forms of mental depression.

Spiritual depression can also be triggered by the denial and/or suppression of other emotions such as anger, grief, resentment or fear. If we believe certain emotions are unacceptable (or even irrational), then we can convince ourselves that we are not feeling them, thereby preventing confrontation with the *real* bogey-man in our subconscious.

Feelings of guilt can arise from the realisation that we are kicking against the religious traces (i.e. our family faith) that are becoming increasingly more and more constricting. We begin to feel guilty because we no longer believe what our family believes; guilt for the hurt it may cause if we break away from the faith. Guilt makes us furtive as we find excuses not to take part in religious activities; guilt comes from having to lie.

Guilt can also stem from dissident thoughts or actions where we have not lost faith in our God or the religion, but find ourselves at odds with the teaching. Guilt can make us slink away from the faith because we feel unclean or unworthy – unable to remain in the sight of God. Fear of the priest's reaction alone is reason enough to absent ourselves from divine worship.

Rejection, real or imagined, is just as poisonous as guilt when it wounds the soul. It doesn't matter whether we feel rejected or abandoned by the religion, or whether we ourselves are doing the rejecting, it is still an extremely painful separation. Something we have followed all our life isn't there any more, even though we may not have actually gone through a physical parting of the ways. It's possible that we have attempted to discuss the dilemma with our priest and hit the brick wall of clerical disapproval.

If the rejection is linked to a moral issue, such as divorce, homosexuality or abortion, it means that we are not only going against the *teaching* of the temple, church, synagogue or mosque. It also means that the priest is sitting in personal judgement on our behaviour and pronounced us lacking – *even if he knows nothing about it. We think we know*, without even consulting him, what his reaction will be to our confession.

Try it now	Ask yourself:
	◆ Am *I* responsible for this situation?
	◆ Why do I feel this guilt or rejection?
	◆ Can I change any of these beliefs?

According to psychotherapists, any form of depression is a state of being in which the normal energy of life seems drained. With spiritual depression it is the absence of that divine spark which transcends orthodox religion and, without it, we become like one of those dark stars – a cold, dead world, still spinning in space, or the feeling of being unworthy of it. Jung noted that those who embraced any form of transcendental philosophy were frequently better able to deal with the stresses, disappointment and disillusionment that life inevitably visits upon us all during our lives.

Crossing the Dark River

The famous 'dark night of the soul' is not a myth, as many who have undergone the trial themselves will testify and everyone on a spiritual journey will, sooner or later, need to cross the dark river. It symbolises a passage between two states, or levels of awareness, and crossing it represents an acceptance of the path we are seeking on our quest. It may be a different approach to our own faith - or it may be a strange and unfamiliar road.

Psychotherapist Anny Wyse explains that there comes a time when the seeker takes the traditional 'leap into the void'. 'Where one lets go of all the safety harnesses of training, text books, supervisors and other people's approval and says "It is so!" Once that moment has been achieved one has a new perspective on life, the universe and everything, which goes beyond the *Hitchhiker's Guide to the Galaxy*'s answer of 42!

'One does, however, have to put up with the disapproval of one's erst-while friends and colleagues. Ian Gordon-Brown used an interesting image in his workshop, *Initiation*. This was that we work or live within one circle of people, jobs, etc. until we discover it is too small to contain us any longer. We have to cross its boundary into a larger, more inclusive world and it is likely that few, if any, of our friends want to come with us. They may well try to stop us leaving, argue that we are 'wrong'. We have to choose – stay and suffocate, or to go on and be lonely, scared, clumsy, unknowing. Sooner or later we choose to move on. Much of my psychotherapy practice was about walking alongside my clients as they crossed this boundary.'

Case Study

Middle-aged Michael is a priest and a member of a large religious family; a position which demands a high degree of discipline and responsibility. Within months of extensive heart by-pass surgery he was undergoing tests for suspected diabetes and no sooner was he given the all-clear than he was diagnosed as having gall bladder problems. Then his favourite sister died; his wife developed ME and his daughter's horse was poisoned by eating ragwort.

Not having the patience of Job, Michael felt that there was little point in retaining his faith in a deity who, in return for his commitment and devotion, had handed him and those around him such a raw deal. He announced to the family that he would be resigning from the priesthood as he no longer felt that he was able to teach that in which he no longer believed himself. The Elder refused to accept his resignation, suggesting that he take a sabbatical and, after a year away from any religious duties, to reconsider his position.

Michael maintained a rather querulous presence around the family, still denying his belief in any God and refusing to take part in any of the seasonal rites that had religious overtones. As his year drew to a close he was one of the guests at a wedding at which the Elder was officiating and he was forced into a situation he didn't expect. As the bridal couple and guests were assembled for the marriage vows to be exchanged, the Elder was suddenly taken ill and Michael was forced to conduct the ceremony.

Afterwards he confessed that as he bestowed the blessing on the couple and joined their hands in marriage, he felt overwhelmed by humility and elevated by joy at the same time. The simple ceremony had triggered a deeply-hidden spring and allowed him to resume his place as priest to the family. Fortunately, he didn't see the wink the Elder gave behind his back to assure everyone else that nothing was wrong and that the sudden 'collapse' was nothing more than subterfuge.

Summary

Focusing on our own pain and feelings of loss actively prevents us from avoiding problems by projecting blame onto others – in this case a priest, the religious establishment or God. Accusing others of having faults that are, in effect, our own, doesn't provide us with an effective method of getting back on track with our spiritual journeying.

- ◆ Can you identify any particular circumstance which could have led to your own wounded soul?
- ◆ Is it important what other people think of you?
- ◆ Does your feeling of pain or loss stem from the sort of person you are, rather than your own actions?

None of these problems is uncommon. As the psychologist says, we may need to examine the beneath-the-surface assumptions of the society in which we live and ask ourselves whether we agree with what is expected of us. If we do not agree with them, or do not wish to live up to those expectations, then we will never be satisfied or fulfilled. The choice of where we want to go next is ours – and ours alone.

CHAPTER 3

Expanding Your Horizons

In her book *The Psychology of Ritual*, Murry Hope offered the view that one of the most profound observations proffered by psychiatrist Carl Gustav Jung was his conclusion that if God didn't exist we'd have to invent him. An observation borne out by years of experience shows that even the 'most vehement unbelievers have been known to call upon some unseen power or hitherto denied force for help or comfort in times of extreme stress.' Or in modern parlance: 'There are no atheists on a battlefield.'

Even so, how do we resolve the problem of reconciling the claims of each of the major religions to be the one true faith? In *Ancient Wisdom, Modern World*, the Dalai Lama suggests that individual practitioners should find some way to accept the validity of other religions whilst maintaining a whole-hearted commitment to their own. 'My way is to understand that in the case of a single individual, there can be only one truth, one religion . . . the diversity that exists amongst the various religious traditions is enormously enriching.'

Similarities and Differences

This is where we must learn to recognise that although there are marked similarities between *all* faiths, they nonetheless differ in terms of philosophy. Although the philosophical contradictions may not be very important in the beginning stages of religious practice, we must accept that culture does not necessarily equate with religion. As we advance along the path of one tradition or another, we are compelled at some point to acknowledge fundamental differences. 'For example, the concept of rebirth in Buddhism and various ancient Indian traditions is incompatible with the Christian idea of salvation. Even within Buddhism itself, in the realm of metaphysics there are diametrically opposing views,' explains His Holiness.

Many people in the West still think that Sikhs and Hindus have the same belief when in fact they are two separate religions. Unlike the Hindus, whose temples contain holy images, Sikhs (like Christians, Muslims or Jews) believe in one abstract form of God. In a Hindu temple the focus is an image of Deity, while in the Sikh *gurdwara* the focal point is the holy book, *Guru Granth Sahib.*

Sikhism

For all the exotic external trappings, Sikhism integrates with little difficulty into Western society although some *cultural* differences have presented problems in the past. There are now three generations of Sikhs in the UK; the first being the original immigrants who had to concern themselves with earning a living and setting up a home. Despite the confusion of identity for the second generation, the grandchildren of the original immigrants are confident, integrated members of the larger community. Dr Sukhbir Singh Kapoor, writing in one of the religious magazines explained that 'It does not harm our children to draw from both cultures. We prefer our children to be married in our own culture and religion, of course. Everyone does that. But there are a number of our children getting married to non-Sikhs.'

In a Sikh temple everyone attending the religious ceremony must cover their head and remove their shoes. There is no segregation between men and women, and there are female religious teachers. Part of the worship is the offering of a free meal to everyone attending and that includes those of different faiths who may choose to visit the temple.

Judaism

The Jewish faith, as defined in its holy books (the *Talmud* is a complete treasury of Jewish law interpreting the *Torah* – Five Books of Moses – into liveable law), is similar to Islam in that it is almost impossible to draw a distinction between religion and culture. The rabbi's role is that of a teacher rather than priest and many Jews refer to going to *shul*, which is a colloquial term for synagogue and means 'school'. Most Jewish men wear a *kipah*, or skull cap in the synagogue and during religious observances in the home as an expression of reverence and humility. In orthodox traditions all men wear prayer shawls or *tallis*, while in the reform communities women often wear them in synagogue. The majority of Jewish families observe Sabbath on a Friday night when the supper table becomes a holy place – a *kiddish*, or prayer is spoken over the bread, salt and wine before it is passed around among the guests.

Islam

As Dr Abdul Mabud of the Islamic Academy explained: 'Islam is a complete code, that encompasses all that affects human life – eating, drinking, talking, meeting people, dress, praying . . . all these are part of the faith.' While Islam is the name of the faith itself and a Muslim is a follower, the word 'moslem' is incorrect and comes from a different root word in Arabic. The Muslim community attends the mosque for congregational prayer although private devotions are commonplace; everyone removes their shoes and covers their heads as a sign of respect. Again Islamic worship centres on the words of the holy book, the *Koran*, and has no religious images on which to focus.

Paganism

Although Wicca is the fastest growing religion on the pagan scene, its parameters are much more difficult to define. Wicca is an eclectic nature-based belief, with much of its lore culled from both indigenous and non-indigenous sources, which encourages a very laid-back approach to the religion. Also under the pagan umbrella we can discover the revivalist traditions such as Celtic, Asatru (Norse), Mithraic, Egyptian and Graeco-Roman, many of which will be perceived to have an almost draconian approach by comparison. Other indigenous religions, such as the Native American, Shinto or other Aboriginal, can trace their unbroken lineage back hundreds of years.

Try it now
For your journal record the following:
- ◆ How do you feel about exploring an alternative orthodox religion?
- ◆ Which indigenous/revivalist belief would you like know more about?
- ◆ Is there a particular religion or culture that holds an inexplicable lure for you?

The majority of world religions are different from each other in that the manner in which they worship is *different* – some of the 'tools' and practices are *similar* even though we don't all use the same terms for them. There isn't, however, an eclectic melting pot which renders all faiths compatible; a religious/spiritual Esperanto doesn't exist.

Why We Need to Believe

We believe because we want and need to. Perhaps it relieves the loneliness of this uncertain universe if we think that there is a presence out there who cares about us as individuals. For those on a spiritual quest it means that we have to seriously consider or re-evaluate just what it is that we think we believe in. Too many people are willing to swallow hook, line and sinker virtually anything they are told about a religion; they will accept as 'authentic and true' the wildest of claims, simply because they do not know better.

In some extreme cases people undergo all manner of personal trials for which they are ill-prepared or ill-informed. One such case resulted in the death of a woman who was taking part in a 'spiritual cleansing programme'. She was found dead near a remote loch in the Scottish Highlands having starved while fasting as part of a cult ritual. This woman had been influenced by 'breatharianism' – an 'alternative, intangible form of nourishment called *prana*, or liquid light' and many evangelical bookshops offer a selection of similar 'biblical fasts' presented as aids to meditation.

In law we are told that ignorance is no defence; in religious or spiritual questing it is also a truism. There is no justification for not going away and reading the small print; for not doing a little bit of research with some decent books that both accept and discredit, and for not applying the same critical eye that would be cast over a financial contract.

If we think it wise to verify the small print on a financial transaction why not extend the same criteria when it comes to something even more important - our soul, our spiritual growth, our ethics and our reputations?

Pantheists say that there is – can be – no fundamental difference between one religion and another, that everyone, however and whatever they worship, is worshipping the same Divine essence – the same prime mover – in the same act of worship. They say that all people, whether they worship Buddha or Christ, Mithras or Mohammed, Herne or Shakti, are thanking the Maker of All Creation for His/Her gifts – for life and all those other gifts which make life possible. Even if we accept this as true, it still shouldn't stop us from checking over the 'contract' before we commit ourselves to ensure there is no hidden clause that we may later find unacceptable.

So there *is* a place for those who believe that all creation and the various forces and workings of nature are modes and manifestations of a Supreme Being(s). There is also a place for those who believe that we reincarnate into a better or worse situation as a reward or punishment for past actions. Although any good dictionary will define the terms Gnostic, pantheist, henothcist, polytheist, etc., it only defines what *styles* of belief exist. What it will *not* tell us is what we, as individuals, should believe: this can only come from within. Ultimately these beliefs are free to be changed and developed as we grow and experience different things.

The phrase 'I am a spiritual being on a human journey' cuts across the dogmas of the world. It renders those false boundaries of religion ineffectual and honours the spirit of those who truly seek the truth without hypocrisy. This seeking is a powerful impulse; it is the pathway by which we move towards it, not the goal itself.

> The religion is of little importance. It is the true understanding of what is beyond that illumines the mind and soul of the seeker. Therefore, that which is sought can only be found within, for it transcends all mundane teachings and thought on the purpose of mankind. The dogmas of the world are but street names for the Paths we follow; a means to an end, not an end in themselves.
>
> (Book of Gramarye)

Try it now	Answer honestly about how you feel about:
	◆ the idea that all religions are fundamentally the same
	◆ the thought that all gods are one God
	◆ the belief that individuals *can* interact with those from other faiths, without compromising their own spiritual integrity.

Our viewpoint about what we see or believe God to be may differ from another's by nature of our background or culture. Buddhist, Baptist, Jain or Jew all live by the tenets of their religion codified by a moral directive as set out in their holy books; and *all* religious teaching is founded on social morality with its roots in the ancient customs. We therefore may have a religious habit rather than a conviction.

The Inquisitive in Pursuit of the Inconceivable

Professor Steven Pinker, in his book *How The Mind Works*, claimed that like the psychology of the arts, the psychology of religion has been muddied by scholars' attempts to exalt it while understanding it. 'Religion cannot be equated with our higher, spiritual, humane, ethical yearnings (though it sometimes overlaps them) . . . What we call religion in the modern West is an alternative culture of laws and customs that survived along-side those of the nation-state because of accidents of European history. Religions, like other cultures, have produced great art, philosophy and law, but their customs, like those of other cultures, often serve the interests of the people who promulgate them.'

Liz, our residential care manager, suggests that if our need to believe exists, then we should view it as we do our other needs, since it tells us something about ourselves or our present situation. To understand them we have to translate the messages sent to us by our needs – so to translate the need to believe, we must ask ourselves what it is we are lacking. Only when we can address other shortcomings in our lives and *still* feel a hunger, can we say we need to believe in order to satisfy our 'higher, spiritual, humane, ethical yearnings' to reach out for the ultimate goal, whatever we perceived it to be.

'All religions have adherents who follow the path of those "alternative culture of laws and customs" because they don't want to be alone,' says Liz. 'They need friends and want to belong somewhere; they crave to please and need to be thought of as "good". They don't want to be different and dare not stand alone. All of these *can* be dealt with without a belief system, it is other parts of their psyche they should attend to, but like food to a person craving comfort, it is easier to take in something ready-made than address their *real* needs.

'The real need to believe is really a need to relate to the universe and, if not to know all the answers, then to know we are on the right path to find them. The real need is for hope, for without hope, how can any of us survive? How could we ever make sense of our humanity, or the world we live in? Because it's part of being a healthy, balanced human being; because it helps us to journey forward; because you can't feed the soul without looking at the menu. Because without it, the soul would waste away from lack of nourishment and, without belief, our potential would be limited to what we knew we could achieve and not what we hoped might be possible. Feeding the need to believe removes all boundaries beyond which lies the universe: the very thing we need to relate to.'

Try it now

In your present situation do you follow your religion because you:

◆ Are afraid to stand alone or be different?

◆ Haven't had the opportunity to study other spiritual paths?

◆ Would be afraid to seek beyond the boundaries of your present belief?

Fear is often as good an influence as conscience when it comes to applying the brakes and not plunging into something without thinking it through. It may be that you just haven't found someone with whom you can freely discuss any aspect of your current religion. Whatever your culture or creed, a sudden announcement that you are about to change or deepen your religion will have immediate members of the family retiring to a dark room to lie down with a damp flannel applied to their foreheads. At this stage of your spiritual quest you are merely consulting the timetable to find out where and how the trains run.

The Religion *v.* Spirituality Debate

People often present themselves as what they profess to believe. 'I am a pagan' . . . 'I am a Christian' . . . 'I am a Buddhist' . . . as though by defining their beliefs they define themselves by a pre-set collection of actions and principles. They move through life applying to their actions what they think *others* believe Buddhists, Christians or pagans do; when questioned they become defensive and argumentative. For them it is frightening and bewildering to discuss the subject on an objective level because many see it as an attack on their belief.

We need to be able to separate our religious identity from our spiritual quest. Often the two *may* walk hand in hand but, in many cases, the religious overtones may prevent the inner transformation necessary to attain our spiritual goal.

> By developing a new spiritual dimension, we are encouraging ourselves to introduce a process of *mental* discernment that will enable us to make a clearer judgement on the different routes open for exploration.

Here we discover that it *is* possible to integrate spiritual teachings from other paths without compromising religious integrity. There is a world of difference between implementing a practical element from another tradition and trying to amalgamate religious aspects from two differing cultures.

Spirituality, on the other hand, is a combined training of mind, attitude and perception, including our psychological and emotional approaches to our ultimate goal. It is not enough to confine spiritual practice to mere physical or verbal activities (e.g. weekly Tai Chi, yoga, meditation or daily chanting), these things alone will not bring about the desired changes. Neither should it be looked upon as a means of fulfilling the inner need to feel good about ourselves which is the core subject for many self-help books and courses.

These inner needs are, of course, important developments but true spirituality is a mental attitude that we can practise at any time, or any place, because it has become an integral part of our lives. Our religious expression is only *one level* of our spirituality; our adoption of different physical activities is another. What we are aiming for in this quest is to develop the ability to project our perceptions away from the mundane, physical world, away from the inner self to explore the furthest reaches of our ultimate spiritual goal.

Try it now	Ask yourself the following questions: ◆ Can you separate your spiritual self from your religion? ◆ Can you define the aims of your spiritual quest? ◆ Does your religious practice satisfy your spiritual need?

For modern people, the consumer culture has spread into the realms of the spiritual as well as the temporal. God and religion are to be bought and sold, acquired and disposed of at a whim. Much of what we read today in books, magazines and newspapers over-simplifies the pursuit of spiritual development by trivialising it for the mass-consumer market. If we believe what we read in such publications, we come away with the impression that our hidden spiritual self can be discovered on the shelf at the supermarket and paid for by credit card!

Feel-Good Religiosity

It has been said that people seek religion as a substitute parent figure and a means of passing responsibility and direction onto another. Both the Anglican and Catholic Churches lost a considerable amount of mystery when they attempted to modernise by introducing the happy-clappy brand of worship and abolishing the Latin Mass. On the other hand, the fundamentalist doctrines of the breakaway and fringe factions have also reduced much of the Christian religion to a mix of 'thou shalt not' and an elitist social club – at least in the mind of the onlooker.

Whatever faith we choose to follow, we all hope there will be our own Road to Damascus-style revelation to confirm that we have indeed been singled out by God to receive a sign. To cater for this need, the evangelical and charismatic churches are only too happy to step into the breach and there are regular 'signs' to be witnessed as congregations swoon in religious ecstasy, and roll around laughing, overcome by the Holy Spirit. Going back to the 1970s 'Christian gold fever' that sprinkled congregations with gold powder, or even inserting gold teeth, spread across the New

World. It later migrated to Europe, along with the infamous Toronto Blessing – one of the least attractive manifestations which causes whole congregations to writhe about on the floor, contorting their faces and 'speaking in tongues'.

Altered states of consciousness

These involuntary states of ecstasy are *not* caused by the arrival of the Holy Spirit but by the transmission of chemical messages from the brain that have the characteristic properties of opiate compounds such as morphine. It has been acknowledged for a long time that certain plant extracts contain opiates that have powerful effects on behaviour, mood and pain. It was a natural progression to discover there was a naturally occurring opiate in the human nervous system that could be induced by clever use of music/rhythm/dance and language techniques.

Naturally occurring endorphines produce the effect of 'spiritual mainlining' and the priesthood who exploit the condition use the feel-good factor to convince their congregation that they have indeed been touched by God. It may also go a long way to explain some of the classic cases of multiple religious hysteria that have been faithfully recorded in the history books since medieval times. Reduced to rolling on the floor by a naturally produced opiate compound would appear to be a long, long way from enlightenment despite the fact that the phenomenon occurs in a place of worship.

Not all reactions are the same. Jayne is a Wiccan who suffered for several years with mysterious symptoms such as exhaustion, muscle pain and digestive problems while remaining remarkably healthy. Having explored all other medical avenues, she was finally referred to a specialist of endocrinology. 'After a long talk followed by a thorough examination, his professional diagnosis was that my increased endomorphic levels were caused by my devotional/ meditational activities. In his words, the altered states of consciousness had literally changed my endocrine system and although I felt quite ill, there was nothing actually wrong with me from a medical point of view. All this is now back under control but it was rather frightening not to know what was causing the reaction.'

Living in a Godless Society

Pushing aside the ecclesiastical debates, entry into the twenty-first century does give the impression of having a certain 'godlessness' in the same way as the old Wild West frontier towns in the late 1800s. With statistics on the increase, particularly in the areas of violent crime, public opinion can be forgiven for feeling that society has abandoned all decent codes of conduct in favour of pandering to the spiritual 'lawlessness' of a desert town where the cult of the individual took precedence.

Any priesthood that encourages blind faith also contributes to this spiritual desert – perhaps through *their* own lack of a relationship with their god or an underdeveloped spirituality, especially where in-depth exploration of dogma, theology and other areas are discouraged. We, the laity, are simply exhorted 'only to believe' and left hungry for more spiritual sustenance. Many of us become spiritual tourists in search of a God we can truly believe in, who will answer all our questions while preserving us from all adversity and challenge – at all times.

The individual has taken precedence over the collective and the majority must toe the line according to the fads of the minority. Again, the ego is on the look-out for what the individual *thinks* they want, rather than what they may actually need. Religions and traditions are passed through with only a cursory glance in the same manner as weekend bus trips that claim to 'explore England'. ('I'm celebrating the winter festival of Christmas, I must be a Christian.') So the ego treks on to another religion that might sort out the problems, tell us what to do, rectify any difficult areas, make no unreasonable demands and certainly never rocks the boat!

Perhaps you have you noticed that it has become *unfashionable* to talk about allegiance to a religion, or even a nation and, as a result, the contracts between deities and their natural devotees have been severed. Practice and dogma have been subtly altered to serve the wants of the voluble, while spiritually problematical areas such as the question of a 'good' God who can allow evil, etc. are pushed under the carpet. We can rail against God, or even blame him/her, but many of us are reluctant to fully explore the issue and have our questions taken seriously.

Followers of the monotheistic religions have seen their

traditions discarded or fragmented simply because someone declared them 'outmoded', and the 'I want' society impinges on the sacred to such an extent that nothing is sacred anymore. To alter a religion or tradition to fit the individual is in effect to start a new sect or schism. We have seen in the past 500 years the uncontrolled growth of Christian sects as each reinterpreted the word of Christ in the manner pertinent to them, which they then present as 'dogma' to others, only to have it again divided.

Try it now   How do you feel about the modern approaches to religious practice:
  ◆ Have things altered beyond your concept level?
  ◆ Do you think we should 'go with the flow'?
  ◆ Or should we attempt to maintain the old standards and practices?

As a result of each schism and separation, we will eventually have a new 'religion' for each person. Except that it will not unify, it will not connect, and it will not satisfy – leaving each soul alone with what it thinks it needs when, from its restricted vantage point, it attempts to see beyond either side of its human journey.

The Cult of the Individual

Over the past few decades the focus of religion has moved from being of benefit to the group to being the tool of the individual. From being a socio-centric safety net, it has transformed into an ego-centric fad which has shifted from 'How can I/we keep God on our side?' to 'How can I get God to give me what I want?' From 'Thy will be done' to 'My will be served'.

Self-help psychology has played a large part in this shift through its emphasis on the individualised member of society. Some schools of psychology teach that all the individual needs is within them and, as a result, many of those following such 'experts' have subsequently become divorced from their spiritual heritage. Such activities and needs, having been portrayed as merely emotional crutches for the weak, have been suppressed – resulting in the natural explorations of the soul being denied and denigrated. Because of such theories, God(s) have been reduced to internalised psychological archetypes to be 'booked for a job' in the same way as we would hire a plumber to fix a pipe.

For practitioners of New Age ideologies the thought processes are a little more insidious. Whereas the psychologist denies the existence of external deities, the New Ager embraces the notion of every deity in existence, irrespective of its background, preference or allegiance. Again, when an individual perceives a need (and the 'need' is usually more accurately described as a 'want'), the equivalent of a religious plumber is called. Often through ignorance, a number is called at random from the religious/spiritual version of the *Yellow Pages*. Once the job is completed and the deity has had what appears to be an obliging tinker, they are bidden to depart until the next burst pipe occurs.

God by Any Other Name

There has been a subtle shift in language recently from the word God to Deity, and for many people this shift is to subconsciously downgrade the powers they are approaching. For some, the word God has frightening connotations – they might have to answer to them; they might be real; they might even have minds of their own and not, as many books would have us believe, simply exist to do *our* bidding!

The decision on how we choose to manifest our spiritual beliefs through religious practices encompasses both ends of the ritualistic spectrum. From the 'smells and bells' of Alexandrian Wicca to the non-conformist, non-sacramental and fellowship meetings of most neo-pagans and the Society of Friends (Quakers) to the full-scale panoply of Roman Catholicism and Russian Orthodox.

This means, of course, that some application of the intellect and physical energy is required. It is not enough to simply read a few books of various (and often dubious) pedigree and sit in a bar with a few friends discussing a new slant on an old theme without any understanding of its true application. The 'how' of a religion or spiritual path may alter over the years according to social events and 'norms'; a manifestation of an ethos may change but that does not mean that we should cease to seek the hidden meaning. We need to re-connect with God on a spiritual level.

Transcending Belief and Non-Belief

What the Bishop of Edinburgh recognises as a fault within the Christian establishment also applies to other monotheist/ patriarchal faiths which deny the equality of men and women. He says, 'Christianity has had too much to do with men who spend a lot of time justifying the exclusion of women. It does not seem to answer women's needs, because it inculcates a feel-bad factor and women spend enough time struggling with low self-esteem.' It is obvious that women's spiritual needs are not best catered for by institutions that are essentially instruments of hierarchy and guilt.

'While Christianity claims to be about relationships, it appears to many women a one-sided dialogue for which the script has already been written,' concludes the Bishop, thereby offering an explanation for why women feel obliged to seek spiritual solace outside the orthodox religions. The consequence of this exclusion has led to many women turning to female-oriented Wicca where the goddess element plays a much more publicly important role. Unfortunately, this has evolved into a bastion of feminism in many groups, which defeats the whole concept of the Wiccan ethic: that men and women are equal – and different!

The constant evaluation and re-evaluation of the soul or inner self is an important part of spiritual development, with many aspects of it transcending belief and non-belief. It is easy to follow the letter of the law whilst simultaneously committing a murder upon its spirit. Each individual will, as part of the growing process, make mistakes and errors of judgement but there is no sympathy for deliberate and malicious deception. The most heinous of crimes are not necessarily those concerning a breach or morals or ethics, but the refusal to accept personal responsibility and consequences.

Re-evaluating spiritual needs

We all act and react according to the circumstances in which we find ourselves – and sometimes we are 'caught between a rock and a hard place' when it would seem we can't do right even by accident. The point is, it is not merely that we do or do not do or say something, but *why* we take that course, and the acceptance of any repercussions.

It is not only individuals who are re-evaluating their spiritual needs. Within the various world religions new rituals and practices are being developed to cater for new needs and communities. These new practices are built upon the established teachings and dogma of the orthodoxy of those religions or traditions, and highly skilled and intelligent minds are put to work examining precedent, antecedent, philosophy and theology before they are presented to the laity of that religion. This is, of course, creating some dissent. Roman Catholics who cannot accept the exclusion of females from the ranks of the celebrants have perforce become 'dissenting' Catholics, or perhaps moved to the Anglican Church. Likewise, there has been a movement in the reverse direction; from the Anglican Church to Roman Catholicism for those who cannot cope with the inclusion of women in the priesthood. These changes and acceptances of changes do not come without a price.

The 'dissident Catholic' has to accept that (in their eyes) the Roman Catholic Church has a personality disorder. While the individual who felt that conversion to another faith was their only option will experience severe emotional pain. Both will soul-search and re-evaluate what they have, what they are leaving – and more importantly – what they are moving towards. Once bitten, twice shy and who is to say that the new faith doesn't have skeletons in the cupboard, or will also prove to be subject to change in those areas that have precipitated the move?

Swapping religion and religious practice is extremely traumatic for the individual involved. If it is not, then the question of sincerity raises its head. Exploration is fine and to be encouraged, but 'spiritual tourism' is somewhat 'sad'.

Try it now   Record the answers to the following in your journal:

- What do I think about self/social responsibility?
- Do I accept that 'with rights come responsibilities'?
- Should my religion absolve me from all sin and blame?

Think carefully before you answer these questions because your approach to *personal* responsibility will eventually become the fulcrum that will influence many of the decisions you make about your spiritual quest and how you will feel if it is necessary to make some physical reparation.

The Spiritual Revolution

In *Ancient Wisdom, Modern World* the Dalai Lama writes that the principle characteristic of genuine happiness is inner peace and that, without it, we have no hope of attaining lasting happiness. Despite the numerous books and courses on the subject, however, this is not a commodity which can be acquired with a credit card and a couple of weekend workshops since access to information does not bring instant understanding.

> Developing inner peace means changing our basic attitude to the way we look at things and behave; we may not be able to change our external circumstances but we *can* change our attitude.

Perhaps we need to re-evaluate what we consider to be negative and positive traits within our daily routine and the people around us. When we analyse the negative traits in our thoughts and emotions it *is* possible to see how they obstruct our ability to attain inner peace. The Dalai Lama maintains that an undisciplined mind is the source of all troubles that do not fall into the category of unavoidable suffering such as sickness, old age and death. 'Our failure to check our response to negative emotions opens the door to suffering for both ourselves and others,' he says.

For example, the most common negative human trait is self-gratification. Some may derive a certain pleasure from engaging in activities that harm or upset others for no other reason than a perverse sense of humour, power or malice. Although initially they may be surrounded by an appreciative coterie, in the long-term, those who have no concern for others' welfare tend to find themselves lonely and miserable. When they eventually find their chickens coming home to roost and life deals them a cruel blow, none of their fair-weather friends hang around to offer any support and may even gloat over the fall.

The first step on the path of what the Dalai Lama refers to as a 'spiritual revolution' is to counter negative thoughts and emotions by avoiding situations and activities which would normally give rise to them. 'To this end, we need to . . . be aware of our body and its actions, of our speech and what we say, and of our hearts and minds and what we think and feel . . .' he says. Gaining insight into our negative thoughts and emotions, however, should be viewed as a long-term plan of action, but unless we commit ourselves on a serious level we will never be able to see where to make the necessary changes in our lives.

Case Study

Sarita is a Hindu, currently studying to become a doctor. While at medical school she met and has fallen in love with Ian, a white lecturer some years her senior. They are secretly engaged and Ian is keen for her to finish her studies before they marry. Although Ian has been to Sarita's home and been entertained socially by her parents, Sarita feels unable to tell her family that she wishes to marry a white man. Ian has no religious commitment himself and is fully prepared to accept his fiancée's cultural background.

A further problem has occurred because Ian now wishes to take Sarita to meet his friends and spend the weekend at their home. Sarita is now torn between lying to her father (who she knows will never forgive her for breaking his trust) and giving up her fiancé rather than face a full-scale family row. She has even contemplated requesting her parents to consider an arranged marriage for her in order to off-load the responsibility.

The ironic thing about the whole situation is that Ian is willing to formally ask Sarita's father for her hand in marriage according to Hindu custom and to bear the brunt of the family's anger if necessary. He has been to dinner at Sarita's home on several occasions and her parents like him but Sarita remains terrified of their reaction. She wants to marry Ian and knows that they could have a good life together, but she is afraid of losing her family and ceasing to be accepted as part of the Hindu community.

When asked whether she felt if marrying a white man would compromise her spiritual beliefs, Sarita replied that they were unaffected by what she was planning and that Ian was perfectly happy to accept her ways. The only advice that could be offered was to allow Ian to formally approach her father – pointing out that parents *weren't* daft and that they could probably see quite clearly that Ian and Sarita weren't 'just good friends'. Sarita is projecting how *she* feels her parents will react rather than opening up to other possibilities and her parents' largess of soul.

Summary

Most areas of our lives have labels. They usually refer to what we are publicly, but what about privately - our innermost thoughts and feelings?

We should reflect on what we *really* believe. If we cannot believe in the whole package or orthodoxy, should we accept the whole item or accept that we are dissenting believers in that orthodoxy?

During the initial stages of the journey we have had time to reflect on where we have come from and why, before we start on the next leg of our spiritual quest. We have now reached the stage on the quest when we can take time to get off the train and break our journey by exploring some of the highways and byways of spiritual harmony and growth.

CHAPTER 4

*We cannot
embark on a
spiritual quest
if our personal
life is a mess.*

Recognising Your Priorities

We live in angry times. As a feature in *The Daily Telegraph* recently observed, there is a 'noticeable coarsening in our day-to-day interactions' with the people around us. The author had noticed a decline in the traditional virtues of consideration and decency, tolerance and reserve, patience and slowness to anger. 'Are we just imagining it,' he asked, 'or are people ruder, more inclined to argue, to take exception, to push, to barge and to make a scene? There's an indifference to others' feelings, a lack of politeness.'

On the surface society has all the ingredients for making life more comfortable and serene but under the thin veneer of plenty, there is a smouldering minefield of stress and anxiety-inducing pressures. Money might be more plentiful but the long hours and unyielding targets, coupled with the need for 'competitive' relaxation, means that personal quality time is almost impossible to arrange. Demanding jobs, juggled with family commitments, and the need to be seen in the right places, often lead to excessive drinking or drugs in an attempt to combat the pressure.

The working day now includes early breakfast meetings before the office. The after-work game of squash is no longer time out for relaxation, it's client liaison. And the lap-top computer means that most of the weekend and evenings are taken up by reports and schedules if the grip on the ladder of ambition is to be retained. Take a husband and wife both working under this kind of pressure and you have a recipe for disaster.

Because of the competitive structure in society, those who find themselves without a job (for whatever reason) also feel the pressures brought about by the increased pace and demands of modern living. We might not like to admit it, but we have become a society in which people are judged not by who they are, but by what they achieve: a society of winners and losers. This has nothing to do with the old class system; this is a new class system created in the 1990s when the goalposts of social values began to shift.

The Chemical Reaction

In *Britain on the Couch* clinical psychologist Oliver James attributes this condition to being part of 'a low-serotonin society': 'At root is the simple fact that while we as a nation are richer than we were 50 years ago, we are by all indexes, unhappier, infected with a collective feeling of unease, insecurity and disenchantment, a lowering of the spirits which finds its expression in depression and aggression.'

Serotonin is the neurotransmitter in the brain that reflects how good we feel about ourselves and the world around us – a natural chemical thermostat. People with low serotonin levels are more likely to be depressed, irritable and prone to loss of temper. Things that happen in our daily lives affect that balance. Traumatic experiences such as bereavement, divorce, stress at work, arguments with friends or colleagues, money problems can push your serotonin thermostat down to danger level. A simple pleasure like watching your favourite team win, or the surprise of an unexpected gift can cause the chemical changes to lift the spirits for a while.

So if feeling bad about ourselves creates a *natural chemical imbalance* that makes us feel bad about the world in general, how do we go about correcting the situation? First, by understanding that there *is* something we can do about it; secondly, realising that we *can* take control. Thirdly, by not reaching for artificial 'enhancers' or happy pills.

Shifting Priorities

We need to understand that there *isn't* a simple seven-point spiritual plan that we can implement by picking up a book and following the instructions. But neither can we embark on a great spiritual quest if our personal life is a mess.

> Our first task on our quest is to establish order and harmony in our daily routine – both at work and at home.

In a stress-related, work-centred society we become trapped on the treadmill of pursuing money and ambition until we realise that 'having it all' is hazardous to our health, career and relationships.

Conversely, the answer is not to believe that to lead a truly spiritual life we must turn our backs on society and drop out. Only a few individuals can comfortably adjust to the rarefied spiritual atmosphere of a monastery or convent – and even those who succeed must still be housed, clothed and fed. As a Celtic *athair* taught: 'It is unreasonable to expect an individual to be overly concerned with the welfare of their soul, the debates of theology and other spiritual niceties when their body is in imminent danger of being separated from it through hunger or other physical deprivation. There must be equal attention given to the needs of the spiritual and physical realms. One must strive for healthy symbiosis.'

In many cases the career, with its substantial salary and hard fought-for position, brings stress and responsibility in unequal proportions. With the constant demands on our time and energy, it is extremely difficult to make space for ourselves and enjoy any well-deserved relaxation and quality time.

Finding time for you

Start by examining your schedule and re-programming it to include a regular slot just for you. Without it being a chore or something else to be slotted in, how long has it been since you had supper with friends or went to the cinema? When was the last time you spent an evening at home with a video or a good book? Can you remember the pleasures of going to the gym or an exhibition? How many invitations have you turned down because of pressure of work or being too tired?

- ◆ If you are employed, study your work-load and see which day of the week allows you to finish regularly at a reasonable hour. Let it be known that you are unavailable after that time and make arrangements to do something relaxing like having a sauna or massage to help you unwind before meeting up with friends, or going home for a relaxed evening. This is your midweek oasis of calm and it's amazing just how rejuvenating a few hours of quality time can be.
- ◆ If you are self-employed, take an afternoon off each week. The world will not disintegrate if the mobile is switched off for an hour's work-out at the health club. Or use the time to visit the

latest exhibition at the local museum or art gallery. Re-connect with the finer things in life.

◆ Trying to arrange some time off from juggling a job *and* children may prove to be more difficult but this makes it even more important to free some time for your own pleasure. Make a concerted effort to find a babysitter or arrange activities you can share with a friend and her children; one therapist recommends hiring a cleaner (even if it is only twice a month) to take care of the more demanding household chores.

◆ Single parents often find the greatest difficulties in 'getting a life' simply because life always seems to be slipping away from them. This applies to men as well as women, especially those who are forced to remain at home to care for their children without any family support. On the other side of the coin, long working hours and a dash home to round up the kids doesn't leave any time or energy for self-cultivation, never mind going out for fun.

It is a well-known fact that the longer you have to get a job done, the longer it takes to do it. It is also well known that it is possible to achieve more in a relaxed and focused frame of mind than approaching everything at break-neck speed. Remember the tortoise and the hare? This is the difference between running on an economic slow-burning fuel or the high-octane variety. 'Both types of energy can get certain jobs done, but only one supports your long-term physical, emotional and spiritual health,' writes personal coach Cheryl Richardson in *Take Time for Your Life*.

Start to look for obvious ways to remove the stress from your life in order to allow for more 'elbow room'. Put all your clocks and watches 15 minutes fast - this will ensure that you are always a quarter of an hour early for your appointments. 'Stop trying to cram several things into a small space of time,' continues Cheryl Richardson. 'This so-called efficient use of time causes undue stress and anxiety, raises your adrenaline, and makes you less productive in the long run.'

Turn to your diary and for the *next three months* block out one evening or afternoon every week that is just for you. First you must become selfish, then start to re-arrange your life to reflect *your* priorities, and then identify and eliminate those things that drain *your* energy. Your one afternoon and/or evening each month is the start of prioritising your life style as a preparation for the spiritual quest you wish to make. Put simply: if you can't organise your day-to-day priorities, how can you expect to come to terms with the question of infinity?

Try it now	Answer the following in relation to your work and home life: ◆ Define what quality of life means to you. ◆ Is there anything preventing you from taking control of your life? ◆ Which is the best direction for you to take?

You *do* have a choice about how you live your life. You can continue to work under constant pressure (in which case your spiritual journey will get shunted into a siding) or you can do something about it.

Flexing Your Imagination

Just because some strange people have adopted new ideas such as vegetarianism, aromatherapy, feng shui, crystal healing or meditation with boundless enthusiasm should not automatically constitute a damning indictment of these. Although a weird selection of humanity has no compunction about endorsing their devotion to psychic adventuring, and the rich and famous are not immune from making foolish utterances on new fads and foibles, this doesn't mean we should close our minds to the possible benefits of such methods.

When the insights or practices of other traditions offer useful advice, it is vital to take notice – even to implement certain of those methods when necessary. If this is undertaken in a manner that does not detract from the spiritual value, then it *can* be achieved without compromising any religious integrity. As the Dalai Lama says: 'Staying within our own faith is usually best because it carries with it no danger of confusion, especially with respect to the different ways of life that tend to go with different faith traditions.'

Used correctly, and resisting the urge to impress our friends with our new-found knowledge, certain practices can significantly improve our universal harmony and well-being by creating the right atmosphere. It is important, however, to be realistic about what we are doing and understanding the point of the exercise without accrediting it with any mystical over/undertones.

Feng shui

Take feng shui, for example. Like a lot of popular Western crazes, it originated in the Orient thousands of years ago, where it was implemented by the Chinese priesthood who advised the Emperors on where to site their graves to maximise their chances of achieving immortality. Which is a long way from the interior decorating spin of using a mix of mock superstition and Eastern mysticism that was picked up by those with more money than sense. In modern China, particularly in rural areas, it remains a custom used by people before building a new house.

Today in the West it is turning into an extremely lucrative business leeching off the house market. In reality much of what is on offer is plain commonsense for creating a pleasant atmosphere in a home. The current fashion for minimalist decor is something that any architect or designer would suggest: to get rid of clutter to achieve the impression of space; put a pot of flowers near the front door; let in plenty of fresh air and use mirrors to reflect light.

Like all branches of mysticism, there is a core of truth so go to the library and take out a couple of books on the subject. Ignore the 'instant mystic' aspects of the content and take on board the *practical* suggestions for improving your home and (where possible) business environment. Just because feng shui is an ancient Chinese practice doesn't automatically make it user-friendly (unless you want to site your burial plot in a strategic position) for pseudo-Western rites.

Exploring mysticism and spirituality

If we're honest, all of us have been fascinated by various forms of mysticism and spirituality such as, meditation, the power of prayer, etc. Ask yourself:

◆ Are there any you would like to know more about?

◆ Do you have friends who regularly use a form of spiritual discipline and practice?

◆ Are you attracted or repelled by alternative forms of spiritual practice?

Overcoming fear of the unknown isn't always easy since many of us have been conditioned to think that much of what passes for 'occult practice' is morally wrong or evil. In truth, the most remarkable thing about many alternative cultural disciplines is their *recorded* success, despite some methods proving to be more effective than others. Even from the most sceptical viewpoint, and despite ecclesiastical condemnation, these approaches have retained their age-old popularity up to the present day.

The Balm of Good Works

One common reaction of those who feel badly about themselves is to become involved with 'good works' in order to encourage esteem in the eyes of others.

By giving, either of ourselves or in the form of possessions or money, we may feel that we are acting in a compassionate or kind-hearted manner to those less fortunate than ourselves. In reality we are attempting to buy the goodwill of our fellows; what we mistakenly see as generosity is self-aggrandisement. Our motivation for kindness towards others should be *natural* and uncontrived but before we can achieve what the Buddhists call *nying-je* (an unconditional, undifferentiated and universal empathy) we must develop spiritual harmony within ourselves.

Case Studies

Nell examines her motivation

Take Nell. She is a middle-aged woman with grown up children and a husband who's supportive and proactive. She is also very active in supporting the homeless. She's always out with the soup wagon in winter, knits jumpers and blankets, and often out at the night shelters making meals and talking to the residents. If we ask her why this is so, and examining the deepest issues of her life, she finally admits that above all (including various health scares), she is terrified of becoming homeless herself. Her father was in the Forces and while he was in active service she knew there would always be somewhere to live. When he retired, however, the main issue for the family was somewhere to live – and employment. The scenario was one that implied ruination and, as a proud family, the thought of welfare assistance was abhorrent. Today those uncertainties are over, the couple have insurance to protect their home, yet those childhood fears could only be held in check by dedicating herself to the homeless situation.

By working for others she was expressing the type of help she would have wanted to receive in that situation.

Janice blames herself

Janice was active in the realm of medical charity. Healthy herself, she had little inclination for charity work until her daughter was born with juvenile arthritis. Faced with a painful and crippling condition and no real hope for a 'normal' life for her child, Janice threw herself mind, body and soul into fund-raising for Arthritis Care, and Arthritis and Rheumatism Council for Research. Her marriage failed, her health started to suffer as the toll on her physical and mental resources grew heavier. When she looked at the situation she realised that she subconsciously blamed herself and her husband for their daughter's condition. Her reaction to the twisted little body was one of guilt. 'I must have offended God for him to punish my child in this manner,' a guilt not helped by 'well-meaning' parishioners who also took the stance that ill-health was a divine punishment for the presumed and unconfessed sins of the parents.

Janice saw her work as a type of penance. Once completed it would leave her daughter cured, thus proving that the sin (whatever it may have been) had been atoned for, leaving her free to return to her previous way of life.

Sarah confronts her fear

Sarah, a nun, spent her time working with geriatrics, the frail and elderly and confused. She would spend long hours at the bedside of the dying, reading passages of hope from the Bible. She instigated a service that created cassettes of Bible readings so that people with poor eyesight could access words of comfort in troubled times. Her rationale was that the last sense to be affected adversely is hearing. Therefore, by providing the necessary equipment, those already cut off from the world (and the word of God) in other senses could still receive comfort. When she examined this she realised that her greatest fear was that her eyesight would fail and cut her off from her Bible. Instigating and providing a new service would meet *her* future needs.

Sarah, by projecting a perceived need onto others and by addressing this perceived need, was creating a service she envisaged needing herself.

This is not to say that such people as those in the case studies invalidate their works through addressing their personal concerns. Simply that through understanding why they chose to work in such a manner they can lay to rest the fears that caused them.

When talking about religion and spirituality it is common to hear people talking about the good works they do, either for other members of their religious organisation or for the community in general. On the surface they are always on the go, full of energy, needed by everyone. Underneath, however, many appear resentful of the time that others demand of them; their lack of privacy; their general weariness. Others in similar situations use 'good works' to compensate for the inadequacies in their own lives.

'I want to help other people' is a phrase that sets alarm bells of a spiritual mentor ringing. Compassion and empathy are not things we 'do' but states of being. Before the physical action is a psychological and emotional reaction; to be fully effective we need to understand why we need to apply the balm of good works.

Reflecting in a Watery Mirror

Regardless of the spiritual path it is impossible to go very far along the road without coming up against the exhortation to: 'Know Thyself'. With the best will in the world, trying to reflect constructively upon the positive and negative traits to our character is like looking into a watery mirror. The reflection is there but the lines are blurred and distorted – while the slightest ripple can shatter the image completely.

One spiritual instruction course includes a question that every student is obliged to answer: 'Do you find it easy to analyse your own character?' A student responded: 'No, absolutely, not! I don't find it at all easy to analyse myself and to be honest I have (until now, anyway) made conscious efforts to channel my energy away from introspection. I have always felt that individuals have a code by which they live. As long as that code harms no other, is honest and generous (as far as is possible) and insists that personal good fortune (whatever form it takes) is shared to some extent with others, then it is not possible to go too far wrong. I accept, however, that 'know thyself' is something I shall have to look at, but it is not something I particularly relish doing.'

The honesty of the student can only be applauded, but until we learn to recognise and accept our 'faults' we cannot turn them into strengths. On the surface this is a sound philosophy but on further examination we learn that the student's approach to generosity and sharing consists of 'cheque-book compassion'. There's nothing wrong with this, of course. Many people give to charity because they are too embarrassed to say no, and however small the amount they feel they have done their bit.

Being a private, shy person, one student exchanged the basic civilities with her neighbours but otherwise kept them at arm's length. Because of the present social climate of being 'bestest' friends with the world and his wife, she felt that she would be judged as being stand-offish or a snob when, in fact, the reverse was true. She simply didn't want to be part of the neighbourhood round of coffee-mornings and lingerie parties. When she was finally convinced that it was perfectly acceptable to keep her distance, and that her neighbours should respect *her* privacy, she relaxed and quickly developed new friendships.

Defining the intangible

The watery mirror also conceals that which we don't want to see, or that which remains just out of reach. At this stage of our spiritual quest we need to put things into a proper perspective and accept that we are trying to define something intangible in tangible terms.

As Chrissie Sempers, our 'wise woman', explains: 'The trouble is that the spiritual experience is highly personal and subjective. It involves an interaction between the physical and non-physical worlds, but to admit to it is tantamount to inviting the attention of those burly gentlemen in white coats. If you talk about your quest you come across either as someone straight out of (or heading for) the nearest psychiatric hospital, or one of those religious nuts who wander the streets proclaiming passages from the Bible.'

Learning to know ourselves is essential in order to *develop* our spirituality, but a lack of introspection shouldn't stop us from making a start on the journey. Every step taken from now on will be directed towards the spiritual goal – whatever and wherever it turns out to be. We must remember not to take things we read or hear *too* seriously. It is difficult to talk about spiritual matters on a mundane level and so the language hovers precariously between the obtuse and New Age vagueness. Neither should things be taken too literally, or we become bogged down with pseudo-mysticism that can be extremely off-putting for the beginner.

'Spiritual quests lead to personal revelation which, in essence, cannot be expressed in mundane words,' continues Chrissie. 'It can only be experienced. And in order for someone to experience our revelation, the other person would have to sit in our brain and see through our senses, while we were having the experience. And they still would not necessarily interpret the experience, or gain from it in the same way that we would. To paraphrase the Buddha: You cannot teach someone else your personal revelation.'

The Finger and the Moon

Although originating in Zen, 'the finger and the moon' can be applied to any mystical teaching. Many different fingers can give the impression of pointing in different directions, but all are pointing towards the 'truth' represented by the moon. The moment of mystic revelation occurs when one stops looking at the finger and makes a mental leap to look towards where it is pointing – the moon.

One major difficulty with mystical or spiritual experiences is how we sort the genuine from self-delusion. At least some of the responses will be nothing more than the product of our own brain indulging in a little fantasy – how do we tell? 'I can only give some finger-pointing here,' says Chrissie. 'Ultimately only we can decide whether to trust in our experience. If all it brings is fame (or infamy) the experience is not genuine. If it tells us how everyone should conduct themselves morally, or in their daily lives, it is not genuine. If the experience helps us to understand ourselves, our spirituality, or the world a little bit better, and makes us more tolerant, indulgent or forgiving towards our fellow planetary inhabitants – it is *possibly* genuine.'

Try it now   Think carefully before writing down your responses to the following in your journal.
- What is the most important thing in your life at the moment?
- Are your priorities what you thought they'd be by now?
- And are they what you most want or need?

You may find that subtle changes are beginning to creep into your answers in the section above because you are starting to look at things in a more objective way. The wider our spiritual expansion, the less likely we are to make snap judgements or decisions. Perhaps the time has come to make a conscious effort to get rid of the accumulated rubbish we hoard in our minds and lives.

Cleansing Hearth and Home

When we talk of cleansing hearth and home we are not talking about a spring-clean in the traditional sense, although most of us would benefit from off-loading things we no longer need. We're really talking about invigorating ways to revitalise our life style and create a new environment. Since few of us can afford to go in for major refurbishment we need to look at our surroundings and see how we can improve the ambience of our home without spending too much money.

Light and bright is the fashion of the moment but whatever your personal taste, the important thing is to get rid of any clutter in order to give yourself more space. Start with all those hidden corners – cupboards, the top and bottom of the wardrobes, the chest in the spare room. If it doesn't fit, it's broken, it can't be repaired, you haven't read it, you read it and didn't like it, you've always hated it, a friend left it behind or it takes up too much room – *get rid of it!*

This is a symbolic rejection of all past baggage – and that *does* mean the collection of plastic carrier bags from the supermarket you're never going to use. Fill them with the stuff you're throwing out and take them down to a local charity shop.

Old glass (from charity shops or car boot sales) and candles are the most effective way of creating a pleasant atmosphere. Place candles of all different shapes and sizes on a large glass tray. Fill a bowl with water and combine floating candles with a couple of flowers and a leaf. Fill a selection of small glass dishes with night lights. Float a single flower in a wine glass. Use the glow of candlelight and no one will notice the walls need painting or that the sofa's seen better days.

A display of flowers also adds warmth and colour to a room. If you have non-flowering plants take advantage of the greenery and treat yourself to a single vibrant silk flower and place it amongst the leaves. Use a tall, coloured glass bottle (wine or bottled water from the supermarket) and place a single flower in one: a single lily stem looks impressive and perfumes the room, too. Simple little touches like these can make all the difference to the appearance of a room, especially if it's the one you will be using for your spiritual exercises.

Try it now	Before you start changing your home, jot down your answers to the following:

- ◆ Are you comfortable in your home environment?
- ◆ Is your home cluttered and/or disorganised?
- ◆ Does your living space need rearranging?

Like everything on your spiritual quest the changes you make are subtle, barely discernible, but after a while other people begin to notice – even if they can't quite put their finger on what it is that's different about you.

Creating a Sacred Space

Anyone who embarks on a spiritual quest will eventually need some personal space in which they can reflect on the changes that are being brought about in their lives. This can be thought of in terms of a private 'temple' where we can just 'be'. Your 'temple' can be in a bedroom, or any part of the house where you can snatch a few moments peace and quiet; even behind the closed door of the bathroom while relaxing in the bath.

The sense of smell is often the most overlooked, yet the emotions evoked by perfumes and the effects aromas have on both mental states and the physical body are well known. It is not difficult to understand that, from ancient times, perfumes have always been associated with religious activities and spirituality. One of the easiest methods of creating an oasis of calm in a busy life is the use of essential oils, or as it is better known, aromatherapy.

Using essential oils

Essential oils are the aromatic extracts from plants that can be used in a variety of ways to enhance our life-style. Depending on the oil (or blend of oils) used, this is a natural way of relieving tension, aiding sleep or boosting energy levels via massage, bathing, compresses or vaporising. There are lots of diluted or synthetic versions on the market these days, so do beware when buying that you are getting genuine essential oils from a reputable supplier.

Essential oils work by releasing tiny molecules that are quickly absorbed into the bloodstream. It is extremely important to understand which oils to use and for which purpose. One of the most effective methods is the use of a ceramic evaporator that has a candle under a small bowl filled with water, to which a few drop of oil have been added. As the candle heats the water, the fragrance is released into the room.

- For relaxation: Lavender, orange, palmarosa, rose, pettigrain, thyme, geranium.
- For energy: Benzoin, nutmeg, lemongrass.
- For sleep: Chamomile, basil, lavender, marjoram, vetivert.
- For depression: Clary sage, grapefruit, sandalwood, orange, rose, ylang ylang, neroli.

Not everyone will respond to all of the fragrances in the prescribed manner, but once you begin experimenting with the different oils you will quickly discover which bring about the desired effect. Keep a bottle of your favourite oil at work and sprinkle some into a handkerchief when you need an energy boost. One word of warning: never use essential oils undiluted on the skin.

Relaxation and Quality Time

Earlier in the chapter we discussed the importance of taking time out for ourselves so that we can get around to doing the things we never seem to have time for. It is equally important to have the odd moment of relaxation or quality time at home, too. It might be difficult but family members should respect each other's need for the odd moments into which they should not intrude. This is where we begin to assert ourselves, albeit gently at first. If all else fails – retreat to the bathroom.

The rainbow chakra

This is a simple exercise to calm your mind or as a quick pick-me-up. Make yourself comfortable on the floor or a bed, and try to keep your mind completely blank for two minutes. Close your eyes and visualise a blank area in front of you, pushing thoughts away as they intrude in the darkness. Begin by identifying each of the natural energy points of your body with a colour of the rainbow: genitals-red; navel-orange; solar plexus-yellow; heart-green; throat-light blue; forehead-dark blue and the crown of the head-amethyst.

Visualise a warm red light rising *slowly* from the genitals, changing to orange as it reaches the navel, through yellow, green, light blue, dark blue, continuing up until the top of the head is bathed in a warm amethyst glow. During the first attempts you will reach the crown very quickly but, as the concentration develops, the light will take longer between the changes of colour as it moves up the body. More effective than 40-winks or a cat-nap, this exercise can be used as a pick-me-up whenever stress or tiredness creep in. For example: an important business dinner after a really stinking day at the office – 15–30 minutes using this technique and you'll be able to boogy all night.

Relaxation with candles

In order to prepare your room and yourself for a simple relaxation exercise – a technique designed to heighten awareness – you can make use of both candles and perfumes. You can buy ready-perfumed candles or use unperfumed ones anointed with perfume or oil. As the candle burns, the perfume will be released into the atmosphere. Alternatively you can use an oil evaporator.

Choose short, solid candles that will not fall over, in the following fragrances:

◆ Vanilla – for stress relief, calming, to lighten the atmosphere.
◆ Rose – to fill your room with love and joy, warmth and friendship.
◆ Lavender – for relaxation and creating a peaceful sanctuary.
◆ Lemon – to brighten and enliven, clear away darkness and encourage healing.
◆ Rosemary – to clear the mind, focus energy and efforts, aid study and memory.
◆ Sandalwood – for tranquillity, harmony and to create a sacred area.

Place the candle in a suitable container and position it so that it will be in front of you when you sit down. If you choose to sit on the floor the candle should be placed on the floor; if you sit in a chair, the candle should be on a table of proportionate height. If you wish to adopt one of the traditional meditation postures, such as the lotus position, this will enhance the experience, but only if you are comfortable with it. Different positions may be practised separately at first until you find the most comfortable, before incorporating them into your exercises.

If you are sitting on a chair keep your back straight, your feet flat on the floor. Rest your hands on your thighs and close your eyes – but try not to fall asleep. *Feel* your connections to the earth beneath you and allow the energy to flow through you, ebbing and flowing as you breathe.

Feel the atmosphere around you changing as the candle burns; becoming richer and more infused with the qualities you desire. Allow the atmosphere to ebb and flow through you with your breathing, cleansing and harmonising the inner and outer you. Sit calmly and peacefully for as long as you desire.

When you decide you have had enough, open your eyes slowly, get up calmly and do not rush about. Be tranquil and you will feel the benefit for longer each time you try this exercise. The candle can be snuffed out for use at another time, or left burning to keep the atmosphere going for several hours while you work, read or relax. If you don't feel any sensations when you first try the exercise, don't worry – it will come with practice.

Swimming with Dolphins

In the caring professions, mood music is used by doctors, dentists, therapists and beauticians to help clients relax more easily. Music is all-pervasive in the twenty-first century but the use of music to calm the savage breast is not merely a New Age idea. Go to a supermarket, hotel, even in the workplace and music will be heard. Why do you think this is?

Factories play Radio 1 to relieve the monotony of a job, cover the sounds of machinery and to keep us alert, especially if the machinery makes a repetitive noise. Supermarket designers know that by altering what we hear (easy-listening music to take away stress) they can affect our shopping habits, or they play music that people are likely to sing along to. When we are relaxed we spend more time browsing and buy more on impulse. If the music is too fast or jerky we become agitated and leave the shop only having bought what's on our shopping list. During the Christmas season the most popular Christmas songs are played constantly to remind us what we're there for – preparing and buying gifts for Christmas. A New Age shop owner has a continuous loop of Medwin Goodall because it sets the atmosphere and encourages people to a) relax, b) buy spiritual books and paraphernalia and c) ask questions.

If music composers and shopkeepers know how to affect our moods, then isn't it time that we manipulated our moods for ourselves? We can either use music to reflect how we already feel or to help create the mood we wish to feel. We shouldn't forget natural sounds either. Some modern composers incorporate natural noises into their recordings: thunderstorms, gentle rain, and waterfalls. Ambient music/sound is a fast growing area that can range from bird song to the sound of wolves howling – and some people swear by 'white noise' (static) to cut through some kinds of tinnitus.

For some, whale voices are extremely soothing, while for others the sounds resemble French plumbing! To some Western ears the discordant sounds of the *shahuhachi*, the Japanese bamboo flute, can be almost painful, but coupled with the natural sounds of the rainforest it may produce an almost hypnotic effect. Electronic New Age music drives some people to screaming pitch, while others chill out with Gregorian chant. Music is an intensely individual choice. Like a lot of things on a spiritual quest, the right one will be discovered via experimentation.

Ask yourself whether you consider these forms of relaxation to be:

◆ Invigorating and well worth the effort?
◆ An unnecessary indulgence?
◆ A complete waste of time?

A surprisingly high number of people suffer from stress, but until they explore methods of controlling the condition via simple relaxation techniques the problem will not go away.

Case Study

When we start rearranging our lives and making space for something new, there's no telling where the path might lead. Carol is middle-aged, single and a senior librarian at one of the major city libraries. A highly intelligent woman, she spent many years reading about ancient civilisations, attracted to the idea of the spiritual aspects of their history and culture. Finally she decided to do something she'd always wanted to do and take a degree course in classical history.

For years Carol had read and daydreamed, but it wasn't until she channelled her thoughts into actions and enrolled on the part-time university course that her life began to change. As her intellect stimulated her curiosity she found she wanted to discover more about ancient culture on a more practical level. She also began investigating the fringe elements of paganism and in one of the magazines she'd sent for she found a small piece about one of the pagan Mystery Traditions. Intrigued, she sent for details.

It will be a further two years before Carol is ordained into the priesthood of the Mystery Tradition but she has found what she'd been looking for through a chain of unexpected events. As a result her life is much more ordered; she has learned how to alleviate stress and take a much more relaxed approach to her daily working routine. She didn't set out with the intention of studying for the priesthood in a pagan religion but, because she was in the frame of mind for making changes to her life, she found herself on an unexpected spiritual journey.

Summary

This chapter has been all about priorities and how to improve your quality of life without making *drastic* changes. We have explored areas that could be the cause of unnecessary stress and looked at practical ways of dealing with them. Gradually you will begin to feel the subtle changes taking place around you as you begin to take control of your life. Even in the most controlled and managed life, however, there must be a goal or dream to make it all worthwhile - so ask yourself the following questions:

   ◆ Is there anything you would like to do with your life?
   ◆ Do you have a secret dream?
   ◆ If you could do *anything* in the world, what would it be?

Confine these answers to your journal – they are for your eyes only.

CHAPTER 5

Redefining Relationships

Relationships are all about how we deal with people on a day-to-day basis. Whereas stress levels at work and home are usually easy to define, personal relationships tend to be extremely complicated by comparison. As a character in an Agatha Christie story commented: 'You can't get away from personal relationships. I've found that in my profession. For every patient who comes to me genuinely ill, at least five come who have nothing whatever the matter with them except an inability to live happily with the inmates of the same house. They call it everything – from housemaid's knee to writer's cramp, but it's all the same thing, the raw surface produced by mind rubbing against mind.'

A fictional quote but it has more than a grain of truth in it. The people who cause us the most grief *are* those we love and often it isn't possible to understand why they make life so difficult. Relaxation and quality time ideally *should* involve a close friend, lover or partner, so that the joy of life can be shared with another adult. Making time for friends and family is an important ingredient when putting our lives in order before setting off on our quest . . . but life isn't always that simple.

No One Understands Me!

One of the biggest mistakes we make is assuming that those closest to us understand and accept the reasons behind our dissatisfaction or unrest. Often we take the attitude that if they *really* cared about us, they wouldn't interfere in what we want to do with our lives. A common student response to how a change of faith would be received by the family is either 'They should understand that I am old enough to make up my own mind' or 'If they really care about me they will understand.'

In reality, they don't! By changing our perspective in the pursuit of spiritual development our friends and family may interpret this as a rejection of them and their truths, beliefs and practices. On the other hand, they may even decide that we are suffering from some form of stress-related illness. As one highly successful esoteric author remembers: 'The family considered that I was too intelligent to be caught up with some strange cult following and therefore it was easier for *them* to accept that I was having a nervous breakdown. Ten years down the road, with numerous books under my belt, hundreds of articles, regular weekend workshops and an interview in a national magazine, they still haven't completely accepted that this is for real. Their discomfort means it's just not talked about or discussed.'

It is important for the seeker to accept that any change on either the inner personality or the outer actions *do* and *will* affect those with whom we share our lives. There is a noticeable change in outlook (the ethics we chose to adopt), upon the calls on our time (meetings, study time or ritual observances), and how we deal with life issues (marriage, children, death and the attending rites of passage). While we are changing our family and friends may struggle to keep up with the newly emerging person – they can only react to what we choose to show or tell them.

Even those who come to terms with the changes, and actively support any decision we make, can still feel disorientated because, all of a sudden, we are not the person they thought they knew. We have new ideas, a new understanding of old ideas, new responsibilities and interests. It is very difficult for them not to feel excluded or left behind. All this will cause a re-evaluation of our relationships, so be gentle. Our families, more often than not, want the best for us, but at the same time they will be fearful of losing something of the 'old you' they love.

Try it now   Think for a moment about those who are closest to you. Would you:

◆ Try to explain why you need to seek a different path?
◆ Appear to bow to their opposition of your change of spiritual direction?
◆ Refuse to let anything stand in your way?

Be careful how you react to any family reservations because it could be interpreted as 'You're not as important to me as what I believe in.' This might be true – but not exactly the most gentle and loving of messages! Even with the most intransigent of families there may be a middle way if only we are willing to look for it.

Dealing with Psychic Vampires

As we begin our quest, we also need to rid ourselves of what are known as 'psychic vampires'. These creatures are just as depleting as the fictional Count Dracula variety and they really do exist. Unfortunately they may also be our mother, sibling or best friend – who would never *intentionally* do us harm but nevertheless are a constant drain on our energy and emotions. If we constantly find ourselves in the position of always saying 'yes' to someone's every request, even though it may be something we don't want to do, then we've found our psychic vampire.

These creatures are life's whingers. They blame, complain, leech from their friends and generally refuse to take responsibility for their own actions or resist any attempt to make any beneficial changes to improve their lot. In fact, they will resent any suggestion that infers their problem is solvable; *they don't want solutions, they want attention.* The psychic vampire wants us to be around to listen to their catalogue of woe, to offer platitudes at the right intervals and to agree that they are just one more of life's victims.

Case Study_____

Anne and Jacqi are sisters. Anne is single and a successful businesswoman within the textile industry. Jacqi, a single parent, has had to give up full-time work and now has a part-time job with a local estate agent. 'Wherever I called round,' said Anne, 'my sister always seemed to be in a mess although she only works three mornings a week. The rest of the time is her own but there were always dirty dishes in the sink. Ironing to be done. Thinking I was helping out, I started to do things for her until I realised that she was leaving jobs for me to do while she trailed around after me, spouting about how life was alright for me, I'd got a good job, etc. She'd find fault with whatever I did and even had the nerve to tell me that it was *my* fault she'd got pregnant!

'I was doing a full day's work, getting back to my flat for a quiet evening when the phone would ring and it would be Jacqi complaining about something and everything. I love my sister dearly but she was becoming a right royal pain! Things got even worse when I met my current boyfriend. She seemed to have a built-in detector that told her when I was getting ready to go out and the phone would ring with some crisis.'

In order to prevent Jacqi's demands from draining her completely, Anne installed an answerphone at home and told the office switchboard not to put any of her sister's calls through to her office. She made a regular space in her diary, helped organise a babysitter and insisted she and Jacqi went out for the evening. Alternating between the cinema, the gym and supper, Anne made sure that she didn't give Jacqi the opportunity to foist any more jobs on her. After several weeks of continued griping, Jacqi began to enjoy her evenings out and, since meeting a new man, her home is immaculate.

By not being constantly at her sister's beck and call, Anne was able to take control and put their relationship back on its old footing. Jacqui is no longer resentful of her sister's career and now stands on her own two feet. _____

Try it now   Identify the people in your life who drain your energy:
- ◆ Can this relationship be managed by distancing yourself for a while?
- ◆ Is this relationship worth preserving?
- ◆ Is this a relationship you wish to end?

Start by informing your colleagues, friends and family well in advance that your new priorities may make it difficult for you to always be available. Remember that the psychic vampire's intentions aren't always malicious. Often they are scared of losing the relationship they have with you and feel unable to talk about it. Others merely take advantage because they quickly recognise a soft touch. One of the outer manifestations of inner growth is being able to handle people without causing offence or upset.

Indulging the Senses

An ancient Indian wiseman wrote: 'Indulging the senses is like drinking salt water: the more we partake the greater the desire and thirst.' Often a partner will indulge their own senses by channelling all their spare time into pursuing their own narrow interests which excludes the other. Eventually the relationship will suffer as each partner moves off in a different direction, forming new friendships and indulging in other new activities.

There will also be dire consequences when one parent focuses all their attention on the children and neglects the needs of their

partner; or when parents are too wrapped up in each other to the
exclusion of the children.

> When we choose to pursue our own interests without taking
> our partner's needs into account, we have to accept that we may
> be undermining the possibility of lasting happiness.

A spiritual quest often means that we get the bit between our
teeth and set off at a gallop, oblivious to the feeling of the person
we've 'abandoned', albeit temporarily. Religious conversion has
had more than its fair share of casualties in the marriage stakes,
especially when only one of the partners takes to the road. There
have been numerous court cases where one parent has disputed
custody of the children on the grounds of the other being an unfit
parent, due to their new-found religious beliefs.

Again we are coming back to one partner wishing to expand
their spiritual horizons and seek that intangible something which
they feel to be missing from their lives, to the exclusion of the
other. 'I *did* try to talk about what I was doing, and where I
wanted to go with it in the early stages,' said one student, 'but my
husband didn't want to know. He kept saying that it was a load of
crap and that I was barmy. I tried inviting people home from the
group for supper so he could see that they were quite normal, but
he pitched in and started verbally attacking everyone.

'The conversation was about local theatre, when he turned to
one guest and said in a very loud voice: 'You really can't convince
me that you believe in all that Buddhist crap . . .' And it
deteriorated from there. I continued to meet up with the group
although they never came back to the house. Since then he's gone
but those friends still remain. The silly thing is, that when we met
up some time later, he admitted that he had felt excluded. He
realised there was something wrong with our relationship but it
was easier to blame the group or the religion for "taking me away"
than to give the marriage an honest appraisal.'

Defining Quality Friendship

Sincere friendship cannot be made to order. Even most
introverted people have a selection of friends of varying degrees of
intimacy; while the extrovert is only happy when the centre of

rent-a-crowd. The term 'friend' may be casually applied to anyone with whom we interact at work, college, the gym, or club when, in fact, they should be more aptly labelled 'acquaintances'. These are people we rub up against on our journey through life. When we move on the majority are left behind while a select one or two keep in contact to endure the test of distance and time.

Even some friendships, however, set their own parameters. We all have friends whose company we thoroughly enjoy. They are usually good fun and we look forward to being with them because their *joie de vivre* adds to the quality of our own lives. We see them as often as possible but they are not the sort of people who become our confidantes. However much we care for them, we know that we could never trust them with our secrets, simply because we know how indiscreet they can be about others in our circle.

At the top of the list are those true friends who can probably be counted on the fingers of one hand. They have been with us through thick and thin – often since school days. We may have gone our own separate ways and probably no longer have very much in common, but the bond is still there. If we want to pour out the innermost secrets of the heart, these are the people we trust not to blab, no matter how juicy the gossip.

When we set out on a spiritual quest we are tempted to talk about it because we want to share the excitement of the adventure. Very few will share your enthusiasm for many of the reasons we've already discussed. Before succumbing to the temptation to reveal your intention to become a more spiritual being, take off the rose-coloured glasses and see your friends for what they are, not in a judgemental way but purely as a safety precaution against any form of betrayal, however unintentional. As a Wiccan of our acquaintance said: 'I'm often introduced at a party as "our witch friend". This means it's necessary to listen to all sorts of inane comments from the other guests and I'd love a quid for everyone who claims to have witch-blood because their Gran reads the tea leaves! I've asked them not to do this but it seems to give them some sort of kudos amongst their other friends to be able to produce someone who's different.'

How do you evaluate your friends?

- ◆ They continually approve of your actions.
- ◆ They're always good fun.
- ◆ They make no demands on you.
- ◆ They never criticise.
- ◆ They reflect your own perceived social standing.
- ◆ They tell you the truth even if it may hurt.
- ◆ It's a relationship based on honesty and trust.
- ◆ They will always be there in times of trouble.
- ◆ You would be there for *them* in times of trouble.
- ◆ They don't always agree with you, for the right reasons.

If you place the emphasis of friendship on the first five points, you may find a considerable amount of hurt waiting for you if you decide to 'come out'. If you don't mind being the butt of their jokes, or the subject of sly whispering behind their hands, then it obviously doesn't matter. But be warned – even really close friends may not be as receptive to your new ideas as you would like, so exercise a little caution before you start talking about the changes you intend bringing to your life.

Oh No! Not the Sex Bit!

Okay then – how about gender compatibility? One of the most significant social changes in the twentieth century was the wedge driven between the male and female of the species as a result of media and political generated feminism. From a spiritual point of view the battle of the sexes has been one of the most negative crusades in the history of mankind since everything in the entire universe is made up from a balance or harmony of opposite energies.

From the universal perspective we have the Sun, which is held together by a gravitational pull that is constantly trying to pull everything down into its centre, counterbalanced by another, equally powerful force within the solar interior which counteracts the gravity. This is cosmic balance on a grand scale. At the other end of the spectrum we have men and women, as different as night and day, but still part of the same *homo sapiens* coin. If we wish to explore spirituality on a wider scale we must learn to look beyond the gender politics of society and religion and accept the opposite sex *because* of the differences and similarities that act as a balancing agent between male and female.

Admittedly this is not always as easy as it sounds, especially when the priesthood is reluctant to discuss gender issues. Despite minor changes, the monotheistic religions remain under male control and even in those areas where women have been admitted into the priesthood there is still a feeling of imbalance. Spirituality is, in itself, genderless and, generally speaking, it is among the Eastern, neo-pagan religions and the revivalist traditions that we are more likely to find equality and harmony on a spiritual level.

Try it now   Answer honestly how you feel about the following gender points:

◆ Are you comfortable with the thought of men and women as equals?

◆ Can you see subtle differences between the male and female perspective?

◆ Do you have difficulty in dealing with the opposite sex on a *non-sexual* level?

Those with an uncompromising chauvinistic or feminist outlook will need to carry out a considerable amount of soul-searching before continuing with their quest. You cannot afford to be blinkered by prejudice or hampered by refusing to accept someone else's viewpoint on the grounds of gender incompatibility.

Coping with Love and Hate

Love and hate are the two most powerful emotions we can ever experience. On the surface we would say that love was a positive trait and hatred a negative one. Unbridled love can, however, be an equally negative trait and have serious repercussions. Hatred for something or someone can force us into a situation whereby we push ourselves into positive action. Both love and hate can be self-destructive forces if allowed to reach obsessional proportions.

One student told us: 'Given her own way, my mother would have smothered me in cottonwool. Luckily my father encouraged freedom and experimentation and, as a result, of course I was going to turn out a Daddy's girl. It wasn't until after he died that my mother admitted that she'd resented his influence and the relationship we'd shared. We got on really well for a time until, for some reason, she started sniping about him. This grew out of all proportion and although I loved her dearly, I disliked her intensely for trying to take away my memories of him.

'I appreciate now that she was desperately insecure and tried to recreate a similar relationship between us and when this didn't work, she turned nasty. She's been dead five years now and it's taken this long for me to forget the unpleasantness and remember all the good times we'd had together as a family. It's such a pity that she felt she had to resort to those tactics because she was a wonderful, loving mother and she taught me a lot of valuable lessons over the years. I just couldn't cope with her possessiveness.'

Although the creed of many religions preaches brotherly/sisterly love, this is not always practical. We can't love the world and his wife simply because we should. As mere human beings, blessed with human frailty, we can take a like or dislike to someone for no reason other than the way they hold a knife and fork. There is a fashion amongst many new-style religions for a kissy-kissy, huggy-huggy atmosphere that quite a few people would find repellent. 'I can be perfectly civil and helpful to my fellow man, without having him or her all over me like a sack of fleas,' said one student with a shudder.

Developing the spiritual side to our nature will help to combat excesses of love/hate and like/dislike because we will be able to rise above the undercurrents and overtones that demand this kind of reaction. In Zen there is what is known as *wa*, an inner peace or harmony that keeps the emotions on an even keel. Spiritual discipline encourages *wa* and enables us to cope with the daily trials and tribulations that our fellow humans inflict on us. Inner harmony produces a hard outer shell and enables us to offer help or sympathy without becoming embroiled in an emotional tangle. It might not be quite the same as universal, brotherly love but it's the next best thing and it's not half as hypocritical – neither is it the same as emotional detachment that leads to spiritual poverty.

The Pursuit of Happiness

We often hear people talk of having or finding a 'soul-mate'. Like many things of a spiritual nature, however, it is a term bandied about by the many and understood only by the few. In modern parlance it refers to someone with whom we have a strong empathy, but there's more to finding a soul-mate than a partner who shares our taste in the choice of petunias for the front garden.

In *spiritual* terms a soul-mate is one who is soul-bound to another for eternity as a result of a series of circumstances – often over which we have no control. This is far from being a romantic notion since we can find ourselves in the position of having to deal with the inherent problems of that relationship over and over again throughout different lifetimes. Soul-binding can be a natural progression of super-imposed emotions usually involving a considerable amount of pain or even hatred. Your 'soul-mate' in this life-time may have been your persecutor in a previous one!

In pagan circles there is a tendency to confuse the terms hand-fasting, wedding and soul-binding. The former is contractual, e.g. a business agreement or marriage which can be for the traditional year and a day, for 'as long as love shall last' or for a life-time. It is a formal promise, usually made in front of witnesses. Soul-binding is a much more serious matter and many members of the various pagan priesthoods will refuse to perform the rite if they do not feel the couple fully understand the repercussions.

Chrissie is often called upon to perform weddings but refuses point-blank to condone the soul-binding rite. 'It's *too* permanent and people don't always understand what they're asking for. Let's face it, most marriages don't last ten years, never mind a life-time. Couples don't get married with the intention of divorcing but it does happen. Soul-binding is the karmic link that lasts for eternity and if you grow to loath your partner, you're stuck with them for every life to come. It cannot be annulled.'

Try it now When dealing with people do you find it easy or difficult to:

- ◆ Control or conceal what you're thinking?
- ◆ Be natural and spontaneous?
- ◆ Put others at their ease?

By learning how to control our inner thoughts we can project an aura of spontaneous warmth and friendliness. This doesn't mean that we must become involved in everyone else's affairs – it would be madness to try. Like doctors, veterinary practitioners and nurses, we need to be able to adopt a professional detachment that people find comforting without allowing ourselves to become overwhelmed by emotion.

That Old Black Magic

Do romance and spirituality go together? Of course, they do. We'd be pretty sad people if we thought that a spiritual quest meant that we had to forego the pleasure (and the pain) of personal relationships, whatever our persuasion. It makes it all the more worthwhile if there is a life-partner with whom we can share our spiritual development, even if they don't share our enthusiasm.

Like friendship, we can't demand love by mail order, although the Tomorrow Project (which predicts what life will be like in 20 years time) maintains that arranged marriages will make a comeback as people turn to computers to put them in touch with a perfect partner. Futuristic dating agencies will rely on psychological profiling to provide more reliable compatibility between prospective partners. And as you raise a quizzical eyebrow, the authors believe that people will become more romantic, more quickly, because even though they have not known each other long, they will just click.

Arranged marriages have long been traditional between Eastern and Middle Eastern couples and now there is a Christians-only dating agency to combat the shortage of available single men in the congregations. Although romance is not the primary reason for going to church, many single women who would prefer to date a fellow Christian are forced to look to other methods for a suitable partner. Those belonging to the older Traditions in paganism also prefer to find a partner from amongst their own kind. And if you're thinking that theirs is a more casual approach to marriage, the Occult Census showed that the divorce rate amongst pagans is *much lower* than the national average.

Love is another country and not the be all and end all of existence. If we have love in our lives then, hopefully, our spiritual journey will give it an added piquancy by making us more aware of our partner's needs. If we are currently alone, the path we are travelling will change our perspectives, so new horizons may open up all sorts of options we would not have previously considered.

The Dying Art of Give and Take

To be in a position to receive love, *any* kind of love, we must be willing to give it. The ego-centric society in which we live can sometimes make it difficult to 'give' any aspects of ourselves without running the risk of having our well-meaning gestures flung back in our face. We give of ourselves when we attempt to communicate our needs and desires to family and friends. We give when we try to help someone out of a difficult situation.

> Try to do just one good deed a day no matter how small the service and see how good it makes you feel. We're not talking about karmic brownie points here, just a plain old-fashioned gesture of courtesy.

Think of the elderly man or woman struggling with shopping as your own parent or grandparent. Wouldn't you like to think that someone would be around to offer them assistance when it was needed? True, folk do view acts of kindness with suspicion but it's only a moment of our time to hold a door open for someone, or to help another onto the bus or train. The inner development of our spiritual nature will also give us a much clearer insight into body language; we will know without asking if someone requires help. The Good Samaritan is a worthy parable in any language or belief.

'It's not just people,' wrote one of our students. 'I was taking the dog out for an early morning walk when I heard the distress calls of three tiny ducklings stuck in the sluice on the weir. The mother was panicking because the little ones couldn't get back up. I had to clamber out on the concrete apron but it was easy to pick them up and put them back in the water. I was filthy but I felt good all day because they were too young to survive on their own and I'd helped them back to safety. This wasn't feeling pleased with myself – it was about having *done* something!'

Giving also requires that we look at other people's viewpoints and beliefs in a more balanced light. Many who consider leaving, or who have already left the family faith, develop an extremely negative attitude towards God. They want radical changes in their own lives but often express contempt or ridicule for those who have no need to implement changes. Since all religions have been 'right' for millions of people across hundreds of years, we must learn to accept that everyone has the choice to follow their own path without hindrance.

Try it now	When was the last time you: ◆ Carried someone's shopping? ◆ Helped someone on public transport? ◆ Passed the time of day with a complete stranger?

Be prepared to do a lot of giving before you're on the receiving end. Professional detachment acts as a buffer against the rebuffs and rudeness of people not acknowledging our help with a pleasant smile.

My Right to Be Understood

We've come full circle with this chapter, because we need to re-examine our own attitudes to the reactions of those closest to us about what we expect from *them*. Since we believe that we have the right to make the necessary changes in our life, should we automatically expect our family and friends to concur with our change of direction without protest? The answer, unfortunately, is no! Just as we believe that if they really cared about us they wouldn't stand in our way, so they have the right to feel abandoned or, in the case of more fundamentalist communities, betrayed. As we pointed out at the beginning, inner changes *do* and *will* affect those closest to us and may even destroy the relationship, albeit temporarily.

'Spiritual growth has its price,' warns Mel, 'and it may be that life-long friendships come to an end because of it. Not because of any dramatic argument but simply because we grow away from people, develop new sets of values or a different outlook which they find difficult to take. Experience shows that this is the norm rather than the rarity.'

Try it now	If there is a possibility that your spiritual quest will take you away from friends and family, reflect again on three points raised in Chapter 1. ◆ Would a change of faith cause a major row? ◆ Is there a particular member of the family or friend who

would be deeply offended by your change of faith?

◆ Do you have the personal courage and strength to cope with such a rift?

Using the candle exercise in Chapter 4 reflect on these questions and open up your subconscious mind. You may receive some startling insights, or it may just give you the opportunity to relax and ponder where your quest will lead.

Case Study

Derek is a highly successful construction engineer with two homes, a racy sports car and a powerboat moored at one of the more fashionable marinas on the south coast. He is divorced with two grown-up sons and has a string of glamorous girlfriends to whom he is more than generous. Despite telling all of his lady friends that there is no wedding ring in the offing, Derek is keen to find someone with whom he *can* have a meaningful relationship.

He consulted a professional tarot reader and was astonished by the accuracy of her reading. A full reading indicated that there was no way that he was going to find the relationship he was looking for while he maintained such a cavalier attitude towards women in general. He needed to make certain changes in his overview of life and to stop looking for perfection in his lady friends when he, himself, was less than perfect.

So far, Derek has declined to change any aspect of his life-style although he continues to consult the tarot reader on a regular, almost addictive, basis. 'I've told him he's wasting his time,' she says. 'The cards show there *are* gateways waiting to open for him but until he develops a different attitude towards people it's not going to happen. Half of the problem is his generosity. He buys the girls beautiful presents and pays for expensive holidays, so they're quite willing to be one of a string of beauties. If he wasn't quite so wealthy, perhaps he wouldn't be spoilt for choice.'

Derek is a smashing chap but his underlying problem is lack of trust. He loves women but realises that any one of his girlfriends would marry him tomorrow simply because of his life-style. He wants a partner who accepts him for himself but insists on dangling his possessions as bait to attract those who look good on his arm. He believes himself to be in control when, in fact, the reverse is true. Because he cannot find it within himself to come up with the answers, he has abdicated responsibility and resorted to the tarot as a means of sorting out his life. In other words, he has not yet learned that to receive love you must be willing to give it.

Summary

Our long train journey has come to an end and we find ourselves at base-camp, ready to begin the long climb to the summit. Here we stop and take stock of what we have learned about ourselves up to this point. Before setting out on the next stage we will have to decide what we need for the climb, and what can be left behind, because there's no coming back for something that's been forgotten or overlooked.

Remember that you will be climbing with a safety harness and that all the pitons have been hammered firmly in place. If you fall or miss your footing, you can only slip a little way before the harness will break your fall. With a little bit of courage and daring, you could soon be standing on the summit of the world, having conquered your own Everest or K2.

You may feel that you need to re-read the first part of the book before making your commitment, or you may be aching to get started on the next stage of your spiritual quest — the choice is yours.

| We cannot build a spiritual life on an unsound foundation. |

Embracing Spiritual Freedom

At the beginning of this book we talked about change and those that you can bring about in yourself. In Cheryl Richardson's book, *Take Time For Your Life*, we found a similar sentiment which endorses that of our psychotherapist friend: 'For decades, hundreds of books have been written about the power of thought to create physical reality. Thought becomes intention, this intention has power, and when you put this intention out into the world, your life starts to change – sometimes dramatically. This is a basic metaphysical law.'

Even metaphysical laws, however, need to be put into some kind of perspective. Most established religions state quite clearly how God wishes us to react to the codes of practice set down by the priesthood. The implication – explicit or implicit – is that punishment will follow any transgression of those codes. Neither does the religious establishment encourage any in-depth questioning of 'life, the universe and everything'. The creation of the soul, its journey through life, or its state of health are rarely, if ever, mentioned. Discussions on such matters, and the publication of material on these subjects are the province of theologians who (in the case of the Christian, Judaic and Muslim faiths), can only 'interpret', or assume certain facts from the details given in the holy books.

The Roman Catholic Catechism discusses some areas such as mortal sin, venial sin, etc., but only in the context of a poorly, sick or dying soul – not how to improve matters. In fact, it can be seen to suggest that at a certain level of sinfulness, the soul might as well be considered 'dead'. It's only when we get to such literature as The New Testament and modern translations of some Eastern doctrines that we see much discussion on how people might manage the health of their souls – much in the way they manage their physical health. The analogies are clear, but the implementation may be woolly.

Mental and Spiritual Freedom

This leaves the individual balancing ethics against morals. Morals are how we, as a social grouping, expect each other to respond and behave. Ethics are what we, as individuals, accept in ourselves and/or each other. There may be a huge gap between the two in either direction as one person's ethics may be more stringent than that society's morals – or vice versa.

Many religions, both ancient and modern, have been used to control the people *en masse*, especially when communication and exposure to outside influences has been restricted. Today, in most cultures, people are much more willing (and legally able) to swap their religion much as they would exchange their car when the gearbox fails. This means that some religious bodies have had to examine how they communicate and relate to their following. They can no longer impose one set of ideals upon a whole nation and not expect reactionary emotions.

If people do not find the solace their souls, minds or bodies cry out for within their own 'family' religion they will, no matter how painful, remove their loyalties and go elsewhere. For that 'feel good religiosity' people will seek for those religions, sects and cults that appear to accept them *as they present themselves now.* Often they will seek religions that do not judge them as individuals, but as individuals who have problems.

The emphasis has changed from:

◆ 'I am a sinner trying to attain perfection' – implication: 'I'll never get there – it is impossible'

to:

◆ 'I am a perfect soul afflicted by sin' – implication: 'I was there – I am currently "fallen" – I can get back'.

Obviously this new approach is deeply attractive to those whom religious society has blacklisted or excluded from the group. Those on a spiritual quest should now be able to view these issues from the new perspective that mental and spiritual freedom brings. For we are no longer bound intellectually by dogma and we can understand that it is not necessary for the priesthood to provide a hot-line to our chosen deity.

Try it now At this stage of your spiritual quest do you feel:

- ◆ At odds with the teachings of your own faith?
- ◆ Drawn to something that is less dogmatic and more personal?
- ◆ That you wish to explore further within your own religion?

Exploring Spirituality isn't about changing to something new, it's about reconnecting with the old wherever possible and developing a greater understanding of those inexplicable energies that drive you to question whatever you feel isn't catering for your spiritual need. No one should criticise you for wanting to follow your faith on a more intellectual or spiritual level than that on offer at the weekly service.

From New Beginnings

In the previous five chapters we have looked at the different ways of bringing change into our lives by altering or shifting perspective. Hopefully the seeker will have found key bullet-points triggered off such thoughts as: 'I've never looked at it like that before,' or 'I've never really understood what it meant' or even 'I never bothered to think about it until now,' because from now on we will question *everything*.

Do you remember when you were a child and drove your parents round the bend by continuously asking why? To passively accept all that life (or our gods) put before us is to develop a Job-like attitude. Instead of asking the 'grail question' of God – 'What does this mean?' – Job sat silent and stupid, learning nothing until even Jehovah lost his temper and gave up on the exercise. The equivalent is seen in the Arthurian romances when the stupid knight failed to ask the why? question.

The true meaning of *sangraal* or the grail quest is the seeking of knowledge. Those who begin this journey are all pursuing their own particular 'holy grail' which will guide them towards their own spiritual destiny. Whatever path we tread, however, there must be some form of guidance and on a spiritual level that will often appear in the form of a priest/ess or guru. Some will feel they can't do with all this, that they don't need anyone to mediate between themselves and God. Of course you don't need anyone – but how can anyone explore a religious path or tradition when they may not know its full extent or what period of study that it ultimately entails? This is the type of information that cannot be found in books, especially the kind that extol the virtues of working with angels and nature spirits.

One student became increasing upset because of what he perceived as a lack of sympathy for New Ageism, particularly in the publishing sector. As he quite rightly pointed out, in every new 'fad' that emerges there is an exotic, watered down, popularist version that bombards the novice with a high proportion of superficial and inaccurate information. Many of the books do contain recommended reading and bibliographies which the serious reader can explore in greater depth – hopefully they may come to a deeper understanding of the subject – but in reality very few bother to venture further.

The backlash is that often those with only a superficial understanding of esoteric techniques start groups, produce magazines, write books plagiarised from others on the bookshelves and generally get themselves noticed by the media. Our student felt that there should be a rebalancing and harmony between traditionalists and New Agers since everyone was after the same goal. He cannot get his head around the fact that many of the traditionalists have taken a minimum of seven years' study to attain their positions, while many of the New Age groupies have only managed to read a commercially produced book.

Try it now	Ask yourself how much time and effort you are prepared to devote to your quest:
	◆ Would you prefer to rely solely on book learning?
	◆ Would you perceive involvement of a priest/ess to be interference?
	◆ Would you prefer personal instruction?

There's an old adage in esoteric circles that we will discover our next teacher when we are ready to receive the wisdom they are willing to bestow on us. Sound book learning is always a strong base on which to build since we become familiar with the 'jargon' but it rarely compensates for the real cut and thrust of an active spiritual quest.

Guides and Soul Studies

Over the years people have come to believe that the priesthood is nothing more than a self-styled channel through which they are expected to communicate with deity. It is also true that some of the priesthood from various world religions and traditions have encouraged this viewpoint. They have done little to remove the misconceptions and even less to encourage individuals to explore their spirituality *within* the religion.

A 'good' priest or priestess – and by that we mean one who is accomplished in their role – is, at the very least, a piece of paper upon which we draft out how we want to approach our deity. This is *not* to imply that the priesthood sits in judgement, or tells us what we can or cannot do. Rather, through their skills and questioning, they offer us a mirror or sounding board so that we can see for ourselves our own thought processes and actions.

As individuals, *we* know what it is we are trying to convey but what we say may not be what others hear. A priest should be a 'debating or study partner', a 'co-counsellor' if you like. The subject both they and we are studying and researching is 'soul studies' and while they (through their own and the second-hand experience of other people's experiences) may offer their understanding of the issue *at that point*, it is not within their power to give *the answer*.

> Sometimes there is no one definitive and unchanging answer to a question. At best we can only offer each other 'an' answer which may suffice until we can explore deeper in the spiritual realms.

A capable priest will not duck the questions of a thorny issue with platitudes of 'It's God's will' or 'You don't need to question, only believe' or any of the other side-steps. If they do, they are displaying their own spiritual immaturity. A good priest will admit to their own areas of ignorance; of their own doubts and occasional losses of faith – and how they re-found it. The most valuable offerings to each other are the failures, not the successes, the tools we used to find our way, the mistakes we made and what we learned from them.

Mirror to the Soul

A priest also acts as a collective conscience. Should one be needed. They remind us, as individuals and as a collective of whatever size, that we have certain obligations if our contracts with our deities are to be honoured and upheld. Should we stray too far from remembering that in our particular tradition, our souls are judged by the best we have achieved, rather than the depths to which we might sink. A priest can remind us that the reason *behind* an action is what our souls are weighed against – and not the action itself. For example, a 'right' action can be performed for the wrong reasons – selfishness, manipulation, etc.

A priest/ess is also a servant, primarily of the deity to whom they are sworn. This means that sometimes what is conveyed to the people of that religion or tradition may not be popular – we all chafe against what we perceive as restrictions, especially if it is a reminder that we are not coming up to scratch. We should endeavour to listen to the message and not shoot the messenger simply because we do not like what they are telling us.

If we are not willing to listen to a priest of our religion, it may be an idea to examine why we are closing our ears and minds to them, perhaps our own arrogance tells us that we know better than they do about our lives. Yet as a mirror perhaps they can see something that we do not. We do not break a mirror simply because it shows the grey hairs! We either learn to live with them, dye them or pull them out – that is to say, we deal with the issue, however well or badly.

The priesthood is also the servant of those for whom they accept a responsibility – a parish, a coven, a grove, a hearth – whatever the grouping may be called. But they are only servants of that grouping *so long as that group holds its side of the bargain with the deity it claims to follow*. This is not particularly negotiable. If a deity has expressed a preference for a particular type of behaviour, and that wish is constantly and deliberately ignored, then why should the priest ignore their God's wishes in order to pander to the defaulter of the contract? So what then is the role of the priesthood?

In short, a priest acts as a mirror to the soul:

◆ As a facilitator and conductor of certain rites of passage.
◆ As a piton as used in climbing, so that any fall is only as far as that anchor point.

◆ As the dig in the ribs to remind us to open our mouths and ask for an explanation, or the tap on the head to remind us to think for ourselves.

◆ As a mentor and (in the language of the Celts, *anam chara*), a soul-friend while we are concerned with physical and material matters.

◆ Or, to use another old phrase – a help-meet.

Try it now   We all need a sounding board from time to time and never so much as when we're facing a spiritual crisis.

◆ Is there anyone with whom you can discuss spiritual matters?

◆ Do you find it difficult to talk about your spirituality?

◆ Does the lack of personal support make you feel vulnerable and alone?

As we've discussed earlier, doubts and occasional losses of faith are more common than the priesthood would like to admit. Often the straying lamb is cast out for fear that the doubts will become contagious amongst the rest of the group and so the 'doubting Thomas' is made to feel as though they've committed some horrendous breach of faith. In reality Thomas was the only one of the disciples who sensibly demanded proof rather than accepting the reappearance of Jesus on blind faith.

Separating the Sheep from the Goats

Although spiritual instruction or guidance from a sympathetic priest or mentor can be highly beneficial, it is an inescapable fact that there are poor priests in all faiths. If you are at odds with your priest because you or a member of your family have flouted the rules then you must honestly consider whether it is the priest or yourself who is at fault. Because he will not give in to your blandishments or pleading does not make him a poor or bad priest. If, however, he dismisses your request without explanation or discussion then you would be within your rights to take your 'custom' elsewhere.

The priesthood is, after all, only human and the ego can elevate a person's sense of their own importance to ridiculous heights. A local wedding nearly didn't take place because the female vicar resented the *bride's* request to keep the words 'to obey' in the wedding service. There were several weeks of rather acrimonious wrangling before the vicar finally accepted defeat and got on with the job.

Bullying tactics and blackmail often go with the cloth. In other words, the refusal to accept doctrine without explanation is deemed to be sinful with the sinner threatened with expulsion from the fold. The worst recorded cases often come from the more fundamental elements of monotheism which object to any form of democracy, religious tolerance, free speech, or the separation of church and state. Fundamentalism, however, is not confined to the 'big three' (Christianity, Judaism and Islam), it also manifests in what are usually considered to be the more passive Eastern religions such as Buddhism and Hinduism. Here we find members of the group being forbidden to mix with 'outsiders' whom they consider to be inferior and/or unclean. In this instance, anyone attempting to leave the group will have more to fear from the priesthood than any retribution from God.

The Holistic Approach

At the other end of the spectrum, everywhere we turn, somebody famous is extolling the virtues of a newly adopted holistic approach to life, health and beauty which offers an inner and outer harmony. Most, one suspects, are merely jumping on the publicity bandwagon in an attempt to make themselves more interesting, 'spiritual' and rich! As we discussed earlier, there is nothing to prevent anyone from implementing the insights or practices of other traditions providing it is done in a manner which does not detract from the spiritual value, or compromise religious/spiritual integrity. Where we *do* need to retain a strong element of scepticism, however, is where we find huge fees attached to the spiritual practice.

Can the implementation of such practices make people any more spiritual? In a nutshell – no. First, we should understand that the study of these practices is not wrong but they are merely *self-centred, physical* activities. They are neither spiritual nor religious. Most are off-shoots of many Eastern forms of mysticism and if they do lead to a healthier, calmer outlook then they should not be dismissed or frowned upon. To develop the spiritual side to our nature, however, we must apply a long-term mental training and discipline – we will not develop this by association, no matter how many Qabalah parties we attend.

We have already mentioned using a simple chakra exercise, meditation, aromatherapy and relaxation techniques but these are only a miniscule part of the discipline required to explore our spiritual self. We may even discover that we have a particularly strong talent for one of them, which encourages us to offer healing to others, but without the private, *inner* discipline and commitment don't let's kid ourselves that it's part of our spiritual quest.

Try it now

Be honest with yourself and record the answers in your journal:

◆ What do you expect to gain from any changes?
◆ Where do you think your quest will lead?
◆ Why do you feel the need for change?
◆ When did you decide to make the changes?
◆ How are you going to accomplish your quest?

Our holistic approach to helping you on your path is to make sure that you don't attempt to build a spiritual illusion on an unsound foundation. Unless you understand the precise reasons for needing to explore other avenues all you will be doing is wallpapering over the cracks. All the questions we've asked and the answers you've given should be offering up a clear insight into the deep-rooted problems behind your dissatisfaction with your present situation. You should begin to differentiate between spiritual hunger and religious commitment.

The Spiritual Sweet Shop

The freedom to ask why? can be a wonderfully liberating experience. It can be likened to a small boy being let loose in a sweet shop – but there are obvious drawbacks. Just as over indulgence at the sweet counter can make us feel dreadfully ill, being spoilt for choice on the spiritual front can also have its own dangers. The question why? may not actually bring the answers you want to hear and where do you go from there? You may find yourself confused by conflicting moral or ethical standards. For example there are several show-biz people who are homosexuals claiming to follow Buddhism; the Dalai Lama states quite categorically that homosexuality goes against the tenets of Buddhist practice.

Many of these difficulties stem from the hundreds of mind, body and spirit books currently available that are only interested in the *techniques* of spirituality. The seeker comes to the teacher armed with a knowledge of the jargon but with little concept of the reality of the faith they think they wish to study. Many approach with a tick-sheet which tells them what they can 'get away with' in terms of commitment. This is why many of the neo-pagan religions are so appealing to the spiritual nomad since there appears to be little in the public domain by way of rules to clutter up the process.

When people don't hear what they wish to be told, or when the reality doesn't match up to the latest book from the New Age shop, they will look for something more accessible. For example, it is possible to buy a dozen books on tantric sex that contain the most graphic of illustrations but very few (if any) will explain the importance of understanding what is possibly the oldest *religion* in India. Neo-paganism is nearer to Christianity and the flower-child concept of the 1960s than it is to the indigenous faiths from which it claims lineage.

'People will always tell you what *they* expect from a spiritual path,' says Mel, an esoteric mentor. 'Having read a few books and decided *this* is what they want, it comes as a nasty shock when they realise that entry isn't handed to them on a plate. Most of the genuine esoteric traditions take anything from three to seven years' study before you get to be a chief. After all you wouldn't expect to convert to the Jewish faith, for example, without a period of intense study so why do people think that any other path or tradition is going to be any easier?'

The Power and the Glory

Those who do not wish to commit themselves to serious study will accuse everyone of elitism and privilege, when in fact the reverse is true. There are, of course, those in every faith whose calling is reliant on the power and the glory rather than the actual spiritual development of others. These are, thank goodness, in the minority. You will more often find that the higher the degree of spiritual attainment the more humble the priest or priestess. This is because the greater the heights, the broader the viewpoint; you understand that the greater the knowledge, the less you actually know when it comes to exploring spirituality.

We, as seekers, must be prepared to listen – although there are times when this is extremely difficult. Again we can find parallels in childhood, or adolescence, when we began to form and express opinions that were diametrically opposed to those of our parents. Hands up all those who, at age 15, thought there was nothing more you could learn from your mother or father? How many refused to be shown how to do something even though your father *did* know what he was talking about? Who didn't ask for help or information because you didn't want to hear it from your mother? And what about all those times that caring advice or guidance was deliberately taken as unfair criticism?

Try it now	As *spiritual* seekers we are barely at the crawling stage. Reflect on your own attitudes to the learning process. Do you:
	◆ Resent instruction?
	◆ Soak up information like a sponge?
	◆ Only want to learn about that which interests you?

Remember that only so much superficial knowledge can be gained from books and if we wish to reach our spiritual goal we need to rediscover the art of *listening*. If we insist on continuously projecting our own views and talking over those who are willing to impart those pearls of wisdom we profess to be so eager to hear, then we will fail to notice when they stop talking and move away. The opportunity may not present itself again.

The Fusing of Forms

As our spiritual inner self begins to assert its influence over how we perceive the world around us, we become more and more attuned to the *genius loci*, the particular character, influence or association of a place which is often described as the spirit guardian. It doesn't matter if it's natural or man-made, a voice calls to us from within and creates a special bond even if the moment is as fleeting as sunlight on water.

Regardless of the seeker's religious background (and pushing any prejudice aside) there can no place more peaceful and calming than an empty church or churchyard, particularly the medieval rural variety. By contrast, there is nothing more uplifting than a cathedral during Evensong when the full choir lifts its voice in praise. And who could fail to be moved by the magnificence of a Russian Orthodox church with its golden icons glimmering in the candlelight?

It doesn't matter whether we visit St Sophia and the Blue Mosque in Istanbul; the ruins at Delphi or Cathage; St Peter's in Rome; the temples of the Nile Valley; the windswept island of Iona; Pentre Ifan in Wales or the fabulous Khajurho temples in India. Wherever we go the *genius loci* can speak to remind us that this is a holy place where we can give ourselves up to the experience and make a direct link with the power of God.

In the same way, we can learn to implement relaxation and energy techniques to enhance day-to-day living. Although the religious establishment tends to frown upon what it sees as 'alternative therapies' none of those included here can in any way compromise your spiritual integrity. The use of soothing music, soft candlelight and perfumed oils are some of the ingredients of romance – who says you cannot use them to help you relax when you're home alone?

Managing in the Work Place

Once we have decided to take full responsibility for our lives and introduce a new regime on the home front, we can take our new-found confidence into the work place. It may be that it's time to make changes because we may also be viewing our career from a different perspective. Ultimately we may find that that hard-fought for position isn't quite as important as we thought it would be and that quality of life is not just about an impressive monthly salary cheque. On the other hand, the developing of a stronger, more discerning inner-self may trigger unsuspected ambition.

Hilary had a high-pressure job in the fashion industry. She worked long hours, was often away from home for fashion shows and frequently worked at the weekends. There suddenly came a point where she started to question the lack of free time and the absence of quality time that was not compensated for by the high earnings. She gave a month's notice and got herself a job as a residential care worker. She now works three nights a week and has time to spend with her dogs. 'I miss the money,' she says, 'but I'm so glad I made the break. Now I have time for the important things in life. Things which matter to *me.*'

The problem with spiritual development is that it is not possible to predict the precise outcome. There isn't a blueprint that will produce a set formula. There is an old saying from *The Book of Gramarye*: 'Never name the well from which you will not drink.' In other words, never say that something is impossible, or that you will never consider doing it. You may decide to stay in your present job, or you might consider your own business or becoming a mature student at the local university. All we *do know* is that once you begin pushing against the doors of opportunity, they start opening for you.

Try it now

Record your attitude to your present job:
- ◆ Do you enjoy your work, or hate going each day?
- ◆ Can you cope with the stress of the work place?
- ◆ Are you exhausted by the end of the day?

There are no quick-fix answers when it comes to earning a living because most of us have some form of commitment, even if it's only to ourselves in paying the mortgage. All we can do at this stage is to keep an open mind about how we will react when changes start to occur. Changes in attitude and perception are all linked to our spiritual freedom.

Case Study_____

Gabrielle still has clear memories of her break with the Anglican Church. 'I was around 11 years old when my mother insisted on me taking confirmation classes. I'd been going to Sunday school for years, and even won prizes for attendance, but the change over to the Sunday service was a bit of a bore so my friend and I often bunked off. In front of the whole class the vicar told me that as I hadn't been going to church regularly, he'd have to ask God whether I was fit to be confirmed and that I was to go back the following week for the verdict.

The following week again he pulled me out in front of the class and informed me that he'd spoken to God and God had replied that I couldn't take confirmation because I hadn't put in enough attendance at the Sunday service. I remember thinking: 'You lying old sod!' I never went back although the family kicked up a fuss, especially when my friend who'd bunked off with me was allowed to continue and take confirmation since her mother was one of the church flower-ladies.

To be honest, even at 11 years of age it was a wonderful feeling of freedom and I've never given the Christian church another thought. Having said that, I think I'm quite a spiritual person and I've found my own path in my own modest way within Buddhism. It also taught me at a very early age that priests were not to be trusted and that they didn't necessary command respect just because they wore the cloth.'

Here we have a classic example of manipulation as discussed in Chapter 2, where someone is told if you don't do this you can't be a member of the group and you'll be out in the cold. It suggests that expulsion from the group and rejection by the priest is tantamount to rejection by God, thereby manipulating fear and need. In this instance the manipulation wasn't successful and Gabrielle turned her back on the Christian church without regret. _____

Summary

Finding our own path can be a frightening step but it is important to realise that abandoning the religion or faith we grew up in may not necessarily be the answer. It is necessary to re-examine (and not for the first time) our attitude towards our cultural and family background. If the reason behind our desire to find another path is due to the dereliction of the priesthood, then it is worth considering whether 'moving the goal posts' might be a more effective way of reconnecting with our faith.

Record in your journal your current attitude towards your family faith. Do you feel:

- ◆ Betrayed by your priest?
- ◆ Let down by the religion?
- ◆ Abandoned by your God?

If you've answered yes to the first question then there's little reason for you to abandon your church or temple since the person does not make the religion or nullify the spirituality of the faith. If you've answered yes to the second question then you must seriously examine whether you've asked for more than any orthodoxy can give. If you've answered yes to the third question you would need to discover whether a 'change of God' would solve the problem or whether you just need a fresh way of seeing God.

CHAPTER 7

Finding Alternative Solutions

Finding a new spiritual path is not easy. There are no quick-fix formulae or rituals that will transform the seeker from one faith to another with the minimum amount of fuss. If we sincerely wish to follow a different religious path then we must take responsibility for our own actions and ensure that we receive the proper instruction before making a formal commitment. There are no shortcuts: our conversion will not happen overnight.

This is where we need to turn to spiritual leaders, like the Dalai Lama, for guidance. Contemplating the adoption of a different religion is a question that must be taken extremely seriously. To begin with, it is essential to realise that the mere fact of conversion alone will not make that individual a better person. 'In such circumstances,' says His Holiness, 'it is crucial for those individuals to question themselves again and again.'

The early part of this book encourages the seeker to develop the habit of self-questioning in preparation for the soul-searching that is required when we begin to ascend the rugged path of spiritual growth. Here we must ask ourselves whether we are attracted to a different religion for the right reasons or if it is the more colourful cultural and ritual aspects that appeal to us. It is also important to be realistic about what we expect from this change-over. Do we expect all our problems to be solved by embracing a new spiritual path or by converting to a new religion that may be less demanding than our present one; that there will be no strict rules to observe and no censure from our new-found priesthood?

It is important to be scrupulously honest because those converting to a belief system outside their own heritage often adopt many of the superficial aspects of the culture to which their new faith belongs. This becomes a smoke-screen, an outward show of an adopted culture to mask the absence of a true religious or spiritual conversion. This play-acting is often accompanied by a need to justify the decision to follow a different path and voracious criticism concerning the previous faith. In spiritual terms, this is counter-productive.

> *Just because that tradition is no longer effective in the case of one individual does not mean it is no longer of benefit to humanity.*
> HH The Dalai Lama

The Need for Change

Much of what we learn about alternative beliefs and practices is found in women's magazines and weekend colour supplements and embraced by Hollywood's rich and famous. Who *hasn't* read about the sexual prowess of one star endorsing *Tantra*, or the latest exponent of ayurveda, an ancient Indian medicine, another dabbling in Qabalistic mysticism or Ashtanga yoga, or the faith healer whose clientele includes an impressive line-up of celebrities and politicians? Not to mention the Tarot, aromatherapy, chakra healing, Tai Chi, reiki, feng shui and colour therapy, to name but a few.

Often these practices are packaged in such a way that they appear glamorous or other-worldly – we're attracted to them by their very strangeness. We pick up the glossy magazines and find ourselves bombarded by articles extolling the virtues of holistic healing and herbalism. Nearly every major showbiz celebrity appears to have a personal guru (whose fees cost mega-bucks) in order for them to follow the latest fad that can involve them drinking a 'soul-boosting mixture of body fluids'. We read that one star favours colonic irrigation, while another drinks a potion of milk mixed with their own urine as part of their spiritual development.

The text informs us that sometimes being rich and famous just isn't enough, and that's why we're seeing celebrities everywhere going all New Age. What the articles don't tell us is that these costly practices are only commercial 'physical' off-shoots of ancient spiritualism. A so-called spiritual healer charging in the region of $100,000 to 'cure' a cancer must raise the question of using a God-given power to command exorbitant fees. What price do we put on compassion?

Exploring the new

The glamour and mystery of the different and new exercise a strong influence over the high-street shoppers who fall for the sales patter and come away convinced that the delightful little crystal will really enhance their spirituality. As a crystal healer explains, 'The buying public will pay any price for a pretty little myth. In fact, there is a theory with crystals that the buyers will not question what you tell them. They listen to the spiel about the great ancient powerful crystal guardian that, by the way, only costs 70 quid, but what price is that for security and peace of mind? Or the lemon-sized Herkimer diamond (a mere £250) that will only work with advanced souls – i.e. basically anyone daft enough to pay the price!'

Many of these so-called healers only have a weekend workshop between them but within a few weeks they have become experts, recommending books left, right and centre and sneering at what they refer to as 'base level souls' with no knowledge of alternative therapies at all. And although the Church of England's recent report, *A Time To Heal*, alleges that the philosophies behind many healing techniques clash with Christianity, you're more likely to stub your toe on the temporal aspects.

Our psychologist friend warns: 'It would be good to think that healing was always good, never did any harm, but that just isn't so. Most healers agree that they are channels for the energy that enables healing to occur. Another word for channel might be a conduit and both need to have certain properties if they're to work well. They need to be

◆ clear of obstruction
◆ big enough to carry the flow
◆ strong enough not to break under pressure
◆ without bends to divert the flow
◆ going to the right place
◆ carrying the right stuff
◆ free from pollution.

'We can easily imagine this analogy if we think of the drinking water being piped into our homes. The same thing applies to energy piped to us through a healer. If any of the above conditions for the conduit are not being fulfilled then we are not receiving clear, unpolluted healing energy. As healers we have a responsibility to ensure we don't pollute or obstruct the healing energy we channel. We need to be sure that we are up to the job and that we are channelling the appropriate energy *for this client at this time.'*

Unfortunately many people come to a new religion or spiritual path through some form of healing process. The 'miracle' they've witnessed over their own (or someone else's) health or well-being is somehow sufficient to be convincing of the validity of the person as a spiritual leader rather than the truth that they are a competent healer. This demonstrates the need to have faith in something, in order to have faith in ourselves. As we've talked about earlier in the book, however, the embracing of such techniques is merely the acceptance of the physical activities, *not the spiritual path itself.*

Try it now   Do you think that alternative therapies and practices are:

◆ A load of rubbish?

◆ Useful if kept in perspective?

◆ A physical doorway to a higher spiritual level?

Healing and alternative therapies play an important role in most cultures and religions, so the reality of the practice is not an issue. Here we must seriously consider the inherent problems of mistaking the healing process for more than it actually is, or crediting the healer with more than his (or her) due.

When All Else Fails

Sometimes, when we've explored all the avenues open to us, it may be necessary to consider taking a different spiritual path. Even though we feel that there's nothing left for us within our own 'family' faith, there still might be an approach we'd not considered. For example, as we have seen the Bishop of Edinburgh recognises the fact that the church does not always satisfy the needs of women seeking a more spiritual approach to their faith. On the other hand, one of our students found herself in the position of not wanting to leave the church, despite the fact that she felt 'something was missing'.

'I'd explored the other religions, met some lovely people, many of whom have remained friends, but deep down I still felt myself to be a committed Christian. I must confess that I was drawn to the female aspects of both Hinduism and various forms of paganism. I realised that if there was a more pronounced *feminine* side to Christian worship, then I could embrace this without any difficulty.

'My mentor suggested that I should seek out a church whose lady chapel wasn't used to store spare chairs and hymn books and use it for the focus of my meditations. "Why do you think they build a lady chapel in the first place?" I was asked. I eventually found a lovely old church I'd never visited before, where the sanctuary lamp burned and fresh flowers adorned the plain altar. I spent many hours there before the vicar came and spoke to me. When I explained my predicament he just smiled and told me that I could come as often as I liked but that I was also welcome at the regular service.

'I don't feel like a lost sheep coming back into the fold because I've broadened both my outlook and horizons when it comes to people and their own spirituality. If the vicar proves to be *genuinely* compassionate and understanding then perhaps I will attend his services. For the moment, I'm enjoying a greater sense of spiritual freedom than I thought possible. I'd got to the stage where I really thought there was nothing left for me in Christianity but I find myself rediscovering lots of things that I didn't know existed in the mystical sense.'

Not everyone can reconnect with their own faith and rise above the doubts and feeling of isolation or rejection. What we don't want to do, however, is find ourselves responding to a knee-jerk reaction and making commitments we may regret at a later date.

Compelling Similarities

When we begin to explore different religious philosophies it sometimes comes as a bit of a shock to discover just how similar we all are under the skin. Most faiths have mystery elements based on the creation, or the birth and death of a holy person. Most have the attainment of spiritual or mystical enlightenment through prayer, fasting, contemplation or meditation. The myths surrounding our cultures, going back to ancient times, all have marked similarities; they represent the foundations of human life. They reflect the hidden depths of the unconscious mind.

According to ex-nun Karen Armstrong, in her book *The Battle For God*, the cultural myth is also associated with mysticism – the structured discipline of focus and concentration as a means of acquiring intuitive insight. The mystic or spiritual 'soul' is a universal currency and instantly recognisable by others who have attained what the Christians would call 'a state of grace' regardless of their culture or creed.

Where we come unstuck is where the wedge gets driven home by the 'word' the dogma by which the priesthoods or the state control the people, trying to convince us that we *are* different from those who do not share our faith. For the seeker on a spiritual quest, however, the 'word' fails to assuage human pain and sorrow. Its rational arguments make no sense of tragedy and neither can it answer questions about the ultimate value of human life.

> Where we have been kept apart from other belief systems due to separatism or fundamentalism we may be overwhelmed by the fact that, close up, the differences aren't so very different after all.

This is not to say that all religions, spiritual paths and philosophies can fit together like a gigantic jigsaw puzzle.

Karma and reincarnation

Many Christians and those following alternative religions have embraced the concept of reincarnation and *karma*, without having any real understanding of the true meaning. Since it is important to avoid the popular Western mix-and-match approach that debases genuine Buddhist teaching, the ideal person to explain this is HH the Dalai Lama:

'Karma is a Sanskrit word meaning action. It denotes an active force, the inference being that the outcome of future events can be influenced by our actions. To suppose karma is some sort of independent energy which predestines the course of our whole life is simply incorrect. Who creates karma? We ourselves by what we think, say, do, desire and omit, create karma . . . In everything we do, there is cause and effect. In our daily lives, the food we eat, the work we undertake, our relaxation, all these things are a function of action. This is karma. We cannot therefore throw up our hands whenever we find ourselves confronted by unavoidable suffering. To say that every misfortune is simply the result of karma is tantamount to saying that we are totally powerless in life. If this were correct, there would be no cause for hope. We might as well pray for the end of the world.'

Hinduism and Buddhism believe that the soul of a deceased person, after an interim period in the Otherworld, is reborn in accordance with the merits (or de-merits) acquired during its previous lifetime. Although orthodox Christianity finds it hard to explain the death of a child, the reincarnationist's view this as merely adjusting the balance sheet of their own previous lives. Some are receiving their reward, some their punishment, for what they have done before.

This absolves God from any accusation of injustice, favouritism, cruelty or caprice, since everyone is ultimately responsible for his or her own destiny. There is a little gem of Buddhist philosophy which says that 'If you wish to know of your past life, consider your present circumstance; if you wish to know of your future life, consider your present actions.' In other words, when it comes down to the question of karma and re-incarnation, it is all about taking responsibility for our own actions at all times.

Try it now
All beliefs have a definite view about judgement and after life. Do you *personally* believe that:
- We have only a limited degree of control over our destiny?
- Our fate is sealed from the day we were born?
- We can change the future if we apply ourselves correctly?

Our spiritual quest will take us into realms where we may either have to change our world-view and perspectives, or bring us up against barriers that we consider insurmountable. The more we understand about other beliefs, the easier the transition from 'I don't know' to '*I know*'.

This New Age Business

A great deal of this 'knowing' has stemmed from what has been collectively referred to as New Age practices. Although increasingly blamed, by certain members of the clergy, for the break-down in social values, this is an over-simplification of the problem as a whole. The allure of New Age philosophies lies in the fact that many still offer the aura of mystery and 'other-worldliness' that has been squeezed out of orthodox religion in its fight against dwindling congregations. The young and dissatisfied needed something to turn to and, as a result of the clergy not seeing or understanding the problems, the New Age has been gathering new adherents since the decline of flower power in the 1960s.

It is necessary to appreciate that this so-called New Age rebellion is not a new phenomenon – every age has had its own particular brand(s) of revolutionary thinking which has been abhorrent to both the religious and social establishment of the time. The first flowering of our own New Age was characterised by the spiritual diversity which appealed to the children of the monied middle-classes simply because of the breaking down of rigid social structures in post-war Western society.

The majority of those 60s and 70s drop-outs eventually became respectable members of the community – settled into careers, married, raised families – but they never really gave up the 'spirit of the 60s'. It became that magical time which the youth of today try to rekindle. Those alternative life-styles and beliefs, however, rarely materialised into something more tangible and, as a result, it is not just the young who are dissatisfied. Their parents also remain in a spiritual vacuum, constantly seeking outlets through which they can rediscover themselves.

The West is now saturated by workshops and courses for crystals and tarot readings; sacred dance and Native American dream-catchers; neo-paganism and shamanic trances; sweat-lodges and dream-quests; tantra and meditation; herbal healing and Qabalah parties; Zen and out-of-the-body experiences. For as Peter Lemesurier pointed out in his book *This New Age Business*: 'Gurus are still two-a-penny and inscrutable as ever, even if most of the 'grand gurus' have retired, discredited themselves or simply faded from the media picture out of sheer public over-familiarity.'

The New Age offered a new age of enlightenment that appealed to both the children *and* their parents' generation.

Out of this Wicca has become one of the fastest growing religions in Britain today, with an estimated 100,000 adherents including some 9,000 initiated Wiccans and around 6,000 initiated Druids. Back in 1989 The Occult Census revealed that there were an estimated 250,000 occultists (including some 150,000 Wiccans/pagans) throughout the UK, in addition to the hundreds of thousands of people with a serious interest in astrology, alternative healing techniques and psychic powers.

Fancy Dress and Hocus Pocus

Summing up the current state of this new religious following, Janval Phagan isn't too sure that many of them have a real understanding of what they claim to be following. 'If a poll was taken of religion in the UK today, a goodly selection of people would now answer 'pagan'. Ask those people what *type* of pagan they are, and an alarmingly significant amount of them would not be able to answer. Neither would many of them truly be in a position to define what the term 'pagan' actually means – though they may have a very strong view on what they think it means to them.

'Most will say something about reverence for nature. Some will talk about Gods and Goddesses, a couple might mention magic but ask them about indigenous practices relating to well-dressings or tree-dressings, charming of ploughs and the traditions of the hearth, and very often you'll get a blank stare and inane comments about crystals and chakra healing. Shame really. Why use the terms alarmingly and shame? Because we are in danger of losing the very traditions and practices that followers of neo-paganism originally thought to preserve.'

When we are seeking a new spiritual identity it is very easy to fall into the trap of what is known in Wicca and Spiritualist circles as 'glamouring'. This is the ability to cast an illusory spell of attraction over oneself so that s/he appears different to their normal or real appearance. 'The main problem with this,' says Chrissie, our wise woman, 'is that you have to believe in it to make it work, and doing this means that the person you are mainly fooling is yourself.'

Unfortunately, many pagan gatherings are populated with people trapped in their own illusions. Inevitably, however, the time comes when they cannot keep up the pretence any longer, the scales fall from their companions' eyes and they only see a sad person pretending to be something they patently are not. As Janval Phagan points out, 'Try presenting yourself at a pub moot (meeting) with the words 'I'm a pagan' or 'I'm of the Old Ways' and you'll be met with the response 'What kind?' It's a bit like someone claiming to be a Christian and not knowing who Jesus is!

'Paganism *isn't* a religion and the so-called pagan spirituality is a made-up notion that all pre- and non-Christian/Judaic/Islamic religions have the same specific type of response and relationship with the environment, animals, plants and astrological cycles. Some who like to think they're following paganism have a particularly sentimental view of plants and animals rather than according them respect.'

Paganism *is* an umbrella term for the various Traditions that have undergone a revival, such as the Celtic, Druid, Asatru (Norse) and Egyptian that are strongly based on authentic historical and/or archaeological findings. Then there are the reconstructionist groups such as Wicca, which claim to follow ancient traditions based on myth and folklore. Regardless of the label and contrary to popular belief, none of the pagan groups condone proselytising in order to recruit new members.

Try it now | Have you attempted to read about or understand any of the pagan traditions? Is your attitude towards them:
- Sympathetic?
- Hostile?
- Mocking?

Whether we realise it or not, many of the pagan religions are formulated under a very strict code of ritual and behaviour which is a long way removed from the antics often depicted on television. Even if we have little sympathy for what we see as 'New Age nonsense' we need to make some attempt to understand why these beliefs have become so popular in the last ten years.

The Fuller's Brooch Technique

Although pagans do not actively recruit members into the various traditions, many other cults and sects do use various methods to attract new converts. The Fuller's Brooch Technique is used by many of the proselytising groups or cults to make it quite plain that the seeker is being accepted into the group, warts and all. Fuller's Brooch was made in Wessex about 200 years after the time of Benedict Bishop. The main part of the brooch shows the five senses and the inspiration derived from them, hence its application here.

1. Instant companionship is offered: **touch them.**
2. The second tool to attract seekers is to provide something that makes the individual feel good about being there. A light, airy atmosphere is provided; perhaps a meal – often in the place of prayer to familiarise them with that section of the building. Few consider the state of their souls when their body is in dire need of sustenance (physical or emotional). **Taste.**
3. The third step uses no heavy incense (to remind them of their past church or temple). Flowers and perfumed air fresheners are often used instead. **Smell.**
4. The fourth is to let them hear good things about how they are inherently good people only temporarily separated from their rightful path. They are given simple instructions on how this separation may be resolved while the priesthood doesn't ask too many questions about what 'God' has to say on their individual case! And don't forget the instances where 'happy clappy' music is set at 72-120 beats per minute to make you feel – well, happy. **Hearing.**
5. The fifth step is **sight**, making sure that the seeker sees happy faces all around. This is one happy family, overjoyed to welcome others into the group.

    These five steps or tools are designed to make seekers feel good about being in the company of other members.

In reality new seekers are discouraged from contact with those suffering with any form of spiritual depression. Practised priests or tutors will separate (as much as possible) the new enthusiast from those just starting out, or those in the middle of some spiritual maintenance project. They understand only *too* well that someone questioning their faith, or the spiritually depressed, are not the best companions for those brimming with enthusiasm. The bucket of cold water that invariably dowses the fire of an over-happy convert might do them a power of good – but it isn't company policy!

The modern way is to affirm: We are nice, you are nice, this is nice, God is nice (if we are nice to him/her). Oh, and let's forget trying to sort out spiritual growth and pruning away the odd bits of dead wood – that's definitely *not* nice! It might all be comfy, welcoming and *nice* but it doesn't support the soul when eventually the proverbial hits the fan and people start questioning: 'Why did God/dess let my sister die when she's only 33?' Instead, the seeker is told to put their faith in God/dess and all will be *nice* again'. In other words, don't rock the boat and don't ask questions.

This type of psychological *shmaltz* is aimed at those who are in an emotionally unstable frame of mind. This condition is often due to bereavement, loneliness, divorce, etc. when the sufferer is at his or her lowest ebb. The seeker on a spiritual quest would go down like a brick in a vacuum at one of these gatherings simply because we'll ask too many questions for which they don't have answers.

Cults and Sects

It's not always easy to define exactly what is meant by a 'cult' or 'sect' when we hear about them in the media. The term cult – a deviant religious organisation with novel beliefs and practices – carries such unpleasant connotations that no group accepts the designation without some form of protest. A sect – a deviant religious organisation with traditional beliefs and practices – elucidates very little response when a group is identified as such. Whatever the academic definition, a cult or sect is easily identifiable by its singular lack of open-mindedness when it comes to an *individual's* pursuit of spiritual growth.

Although the media like to label occult groups as cults or sects, the vast majority of those who find themselves on the sharp end of media attention are those with a Christian slant. As have those mass-deaths that have reached horror-movie proportions in America, Guyana, Africa, Switzerland and Canada. Cults and sects usually expect members to hand over all financial assets and use techniques of influence both to recruit and retain members.

Again the lack of spiritual freedom would make this a no-go area for a genuine seeker. It is easy to make the mistake of going along to find out more about such groups with a view to greater understanding, especially when the recruiting officers are likeable, plausible people who talk easily about the lack of social obligation, how consumerism is polluting our standards and how the group aims to reintroduce old traditions and values. Would that type of sales patter convince you to go along and hear what they've got to say with an open mind, avoid them like the plague or intrigue you to the point where you couldn't stay away?

Whether we like it or not, the status quo *is* being changed.

> Tired of mere consumerism and the transient nature of most consumer goods, some people are now thirsty for something more permanent, life changing and personal.

People understand the dangers inherent in knowing the price of everything and the value of nothing, and actively seek something that will satisfy their hunger, give meaning to their lives and at least have a hint that this physical life is not all that there is. Often these are the very people who fall prey to a cult or sect on a recruiting drive.

Choosing the Path

Many people ask if we choose our path or our path chooses us. Here we must examine our own commitment to our spiritual quest. For some the journey is a curiosity and an extension of perspective. Others would find it easier to cease breathing than to give up their quest because they have looked at all the other avenues and accepted the challenges their chosen path offers. Some people consciously or sub-consciously look for patterns within what they see and experience. They search for 'like', while others look for the differences and the 'unlike'.

This means that some move to another religion or practice because they wish their existing world-view to be confirmed – they already believe that life and death has certain meaning, and ways of being dealt with. These people will search until they find a path that tells them what they feel they already know 'in their water'. Others will examine the path, see how it is different from others, how it challenges their existing world-view and move towards the one that appears to expand their parameters. This is similar to the differences posed by the complementary questions of why and why not?

Another of our colleagues responded by quoting the old adage 'Good cooks are born not made' and this can sometimes also be applied to our own spiritual path. I have known people go through the initiatory ranks of supposedly spiritual institutions as if they were simply taking a set of exams. They have not grasped that spiritual awareness is not about passing exams, no matter how high you climb in an institution. Whether it is through the ranks of the Church, or any other spiritual hierarchy, if you are not *living* that faith you are not following its true spiritual tenets.

An old Buddhist joke tells of the pupil who asked his teacher who was the most advanced soul in the room, expecting to be picked out because of his scholarly knowledge. After careful consideration the teacher turned and bowed to a cat asleep by the fire. The cat was being true to its own path and not pretending to be something it was not.

We cannot advance spiritually by passing exams, nor can we call ourselves a member of any religion unless we practise that religion and believe in it – paying lip service does not count.

It may be, however, that you are so in tune with a particular path that there simply is no choice. A cat cannot become a dog, no matter how much it wants to – a cat will always be a cat. But it can choose what *kind* of cat it is. So you too may find that there really is no choice for you on your spiritual path; you may *have* to take a certain course. Even so, there are always choices you can make about the manner in which you will travel your path – what you will emphasise, what you will minimise, how deeply (or not) you immerse yourself in its application. And – most important of all – how you achieve the balance between the needs and compulsions of your spiritual path and the necessities of the society in which you live.

The Need for Discernment

On the spiritual path the seeker needs a healthy degree of scepticism and discernment because never has the fight for your soul been so public. Religion is big business nowadays, as any trip to a bookshop will quickly prove. Wherever we look, there are books on paganism, New Age healing techniques, ancient religions and cultures, self-help, colour therapies and more. At every opportunity someone is saying: 'This is the way to be; this is what you should believe in; this is the answer to all of your problems.'

Put on the radio (especially Radios 3 and 4) and there's usually a debate somewhere in the day's programme pitting science against spirituality. Television broadcasts *The God Channel*, *Christian Music* and religious programmes from around the world, bringing images of various forms of worship into our homes. Along with the self-help books, the 'only believe in God' promises of the TV channels, the deep debates on the radio, the fight for the soul is manifesting in the arts. We have spiritual poetry and dance, music and song; not to mention the seductive invitation to come and see what that the dancer, song-writer or poet glimpsed in a moment of heightened awareness.

Yet even with the publications, programmes and arts showing various 'ways of being', the majority of seekers are still not happy. In the search for enlightenment and sifting through the promises and book titles, they overlook one important fact – enlightenment does *not* promise happiness or bring joy; it merely brings enlightenment. The second-hand sharing of experiences via the various media are only sepia-coloured images seen as just more fleeting landscapes through the windows of our speeding train.

Learning to differentiate

Slipping and sliding between history and myth is another area where the seeker must learn to differentiate. The Bishop of Edinburgh himself warns about the dangers of taking ancient myth literally, giving as an example the way in which Christianity has allowed itself to be imprisoned by its own lack of historical imagination and versatility in interpreting ancient texts.

'There is,' he explains, 'an inescapable tendency to solidify our experiments into traditions, to establish them as normative, so that they guarantee our automatic consent . . .' Traditions can only work as long as they operate in this subliminal way; they fail when people openly begin to question and consciously withdraw their support or consent. This disintegration happens when the tradition refuses to move with the times and erodes the original context that gave it power and plausibility.

Amongst modern pagan religions there is a tendency to attempt the inauguration of *new* traditions while desperately striving towards trying to establish them as having traceable antecedents. Often we find tenuous historical lineage being claimed to give the tradition (and its founders) some form of credibility. Few of these new groups can pass muster and quickly disappear – usually in a cloud of acrimony and bad feeling.

Try it now	Before making contact with any religious or spiritual grouping, ask yourself the following because your well-being might depend on the answers:

- Have you checked out the background of the group?
- Do you know the *right* questions to ask?
- Are you prepared for a swift exit if you get the wrong answers?

Although it may feel wrong to be suspicious when we're discussing spirituality, it's a fact of life that there are plenty of strange people out there hiding under the mantel of guru and spiritual teacher. Announcements by religious groups often appear in magazines, newsletters and newspapers and while most of these entries are probably reputable, not all will be. If there is any doubt, it is often useful to ask the editor of such publications if they personally know of the individual or group concerned.

The Meeting Place

Should you decide to meet strangers as part of your spiritual quest, always arrange a meeting on neutral ground – a café, a restaurant or quiet pub bar is ideal. If you don't like the look of them (or they of you), either party can leave without causing offence. Such a meeting also prevents the awkwardness of 'official' interviews, when both parties know that the meeting has come to an end but cannot find the right words with which to end it. Never arrange secret meetings in unknown places. If necessary take your partner or a friend if you wish – they can always keep an eye on proceedings from a discreet distance, though not necessarily in a position to overhear the conversation.

Regardless of the religious or spiritual nature of the group, make sure you have your own list along the following lines:

- ◆ What type of group is involved: training, working or mixed?
- ◆ What exact tradition or path does it follow?
- ◆ How often does the group meet?
- ◆ Does it meet in someone's house; are there any house rules to be aware of, e.g. cigarettes or vegetarian food, time of arrival before the meeting starts, etc? (Here we stress the importance of not going into someone's house until you feel comfortable about doing so. Neither should you invite them to your home until you're comfortable with them.)
- ◆ How long are the meetings? (Always let someone know where you are and the time you're expected home.)
- ◆ Is there a required reading list?
- ◆ In the case of esoteric groups check on the clothing worn for a meeting. Are robes bought or made, and by whom?
- ◆ Is there a monetary fee involved; how much is it and when payable?
- ◆ Is a contribution towards refreshments required, and in what form, money or pot luck?
- ◆ What are the group's 'entry' requirements?
- ◆ Last and most important: *never under any circumstances accept the offer of a lift home.*

The spiritual quest comes with its own set of dangers as a concerted read of the less sensational newspapers will testify. Don't allow your enthusiasm for the journey cloud your commonsense.

Case Study_____

In her own inimitable style of taking things to extremes, Chrissie felt compelled to explore all avenues of faith before turning to paganism. 'I had felt drawn to a form of more nature-based worship from an early age – to be honest for as long as I could remember. When other kids talked about becoming doctors or teachers, the only thing I wanted when I grew up was to become one with the spirit I felt enlivened this planet – I suppose it is what has become known as the Gaia principle.'

Brought up in a Christian household (her father's family was Catholic), Chrissie attended church regularly, enjoying the singing, even the difficult psalms, and often used to read the lessons from the Bible. She went to Sunday school, helped in cleaning and decorating the church and handing out prayer books. By the age of 14 she had been confirmed but still retained a strong interest in paganism.

Leaving school, she went to work as a clerk in a local factory.

Her interests were still very wide and she found she needed to develop the spiritual side of her life, and so read everything she could on alternative religions while still attending church regularly. Nothing undermined her fascination with nature-based worship but by then she understood that, from the church's point of view, Craft practice was not seen as compatible with a Christian way of life.

'I believed then, as I do now, that all religions are merely expressions of the same striving for understanding and contact with the ultimate source of universal being. Having been brought up as a Christian I felt that before I could reject Christianity as being the right spiritual path for me, I had to give it the best possible chance. I had to immerse myself in it, study it and live the Christian life. And the best way for me to do this was to test my vocation in a convent - so I became a nun.

'That didn't last long – I soon discovered that the contradictions I had found mildly annoying as an ordinary churchgoer became huge sticking points, massive obstacles that I was forced to beat my head and my faith against. I was soon home again but I'd done my best by Christianity and felt free to move away from it and pursue my need and desire to explore my own path. I immersed myself in the spiritual life I felt to be all around me and expressed in every aspect of this beautiful planet, not just in the way that humans relate to one another.'

During the intervening years Chrissie has become acknowledged both as a practitioner of paganism and as an inspirational teacher, often consulted by writers seeking alternative spiritual insights. _____

Summary

If you find as a result of long and hard deliberation that you are unable to reconnect with your faith, there are many alternatives for you to explore. Bear in mind, however, that the spark of spirituality that burns deep inside everyone will guide you to the 'chosen' path when the time is right. You just might not have a say in the 'choosing'.

The late Doreen Valiente, herself a respected Wiccan high priestess wrote: 'If that which thou seekest, thou findest not within thee, then thou wilt never find it without thee.'

Learn about a
pine tree from
a pine tree,
about a
bamboo from a
bamboo.

CHAPTER 8

Bringing About Change

At the start of this book we introduced the concept that we cannot change anything but ourselves, but in changing ourselves we will find the world changes around us. In subsequent chapters we have explored the options open to us and made suggestions of what we might consider to help us achieve our spiritual goal. We've shown how we can use the tools to help make the application easier. Now we face the challenge of implementing these suggestions in order to bring about any changes we feel we need for self-improvement.

We began with a gentle learning curve that encouraged the examination of different faiths and cultures in order to develop a world-view of belief and recognise the differences and similarities. Learning and the acquisition of knowledge alone, however, are not sufficient. There are those who absorb information and set themselves up as teachers without actually practising what they preach because they lack the commitment to *actively* set out on a spiritual quest themselves. Like the conductor or driver of a train: they travel the route but never disembark at the destination. These are the next steps:

◆ We need to develop the **conviction** that we are committed to this spiritual journey; that it is not just a brief excursion but a quest that may take the rest of our lives. It is probably at this stage that we will come up against the opposition of our friends and family, who will resort to all sorts of tricks to undermine our resolve. This is just one of the first tests we will experience along the way.

◆ With the additional strength of **determination**, however, we can overcome these barriers even at the possible cost of giving offence. Once we have begun to take those first, tottering steps along the path of our choice, we will begin to feel the courage of our convictions pushing us forward with a sense of determination to succeed by increasing our awareness of what we *can* achieve.

◆ Transforming determination into **action** moves our spiritual quest from the realms of the 'if-only' or intellect, into the glare of reality. This is our 'coming out' whereby we begin to live our life under a new set of spiritual guidelines.

◆ Only sustained **effort** can implement the actual changes. These changes must become a way of life in order to overcome any form of negative residue from a wounded soul. It is important, however, to understand that these inner changes will not take place overnight, our spiritual observances need time to acquire their own habit patterns.

As Dr Cutler observes in *The Art of Happiness*, this method is in sharp contrast to the proliferation of quick-fix, self-help techniques that have become so popular in Western culture in recent decades – ranging from 'positive affirmations' to 'discovering the inner child'. The real answer to the question of how long is a spiritual journey is as long as it takes. This doesn't mean a weekend workshop or the completion of a distance learning course since these are mere signposts along the way. Neither does it mean drawing information from any source without checking its authenticity. As the Japanese writer Basho tells us: 'Learn about a pine tree from a pine tree, and about a bamboo plant from a bamboo.' While there are hundreds of books in the mind, body and spirit genre written by 'nice' people whose view of spirituality is 'nice', it does not mean that they have lived the spirituality they publish. They may offer information but not understanding. 'Nice', 'quick', 'easy' or 'simple' does not mean 'understood', 'effective' or 'permanent'.

Exercising Your Mind

The real breakthrough on the spiritual path is the ability to view God without the trappings of religion. That is to say, accepting the Divine Power (however we choose to see it) without it being decked out in the persona of a benign or bad-tempered patriarch, an archetypal hunter, a universal mother or a divine child. Whatever the faith or belief, religious myths, parables and stories were the teaching tools of the priesthood in a time when the vast majority of the populace (even the nobility) were illiterate.

To teach the message of God, some priestly artists concocted a picture-book style of instruction. God and his extended family/court took on preprescribed images that were instantly recognisable to even the dumbest tribal member. Their adventures, battles and triumphs evolved into the fundamental truths of the religion and passed into the collective consciousness of the human race across the globe. This progress is recorded in the world's finest collections of religious art and, as seekers of spiritual enlightenment, we would do well to reflect on these images as part of our inner development.

As the human race became more sophisticated in its pursuit of religious expression, so the vast temples dominated the landscape, firmly stamping the 'word' in stone. By reducing God to a mere cipher, the priesthood expanded its own control over people's thinking. God tells us what to do via the priesthood and there's all hell to pay if we suddenly decide to wake up and smell the roses. As spiritual seekers, however, we *must* learn to wake up and discover this other side of God for ourselves.

Try it now

Put the following in your list of things to do:

- ◆ Visit the local museum or art gallery and reflect on the religious art (ancient and modern) in the collection.
- ◆ Read at least one book on the mysticism of one of the major religions other than your own.
- ◆ Visit at least one sacred site (ancient or modern) and view it with an open mind and heart.
- ◆ Visit at least one natural beauty spot for the purpose of meditation and reflection.

These simple exercises help us to cut through the fundamental red-tape of dogma and separate the myth from ideology. Without this separation it is easy to lose sight of the whole tradition of spirituality by suppressing intuitive mysticism and what Karen Armstrong describes as 'the unconscious, deeper impulses of the personality.'

Meditating on the Future

The key to all spiritual development is, of course, the eternal question of what becomes of us when we die. Contemplating the future means accepting the reality of our own death and the deaths of those we love. But what happens to us after death? Because of the conflicting religious philosophies, there is more confusion than comfort – and, as we've discussed earlier, very often the wounded soul condition comes about *as a result* of bereavement.

'Death is not a negotiable asset,' says Mel, a spiritual mentor, 'and yet those who have attained a certain level of spiritual awareness no longer fear death, only the *manner* of their passing. This sounds like a cliché but death really is only another gateway. This doesn't mean we should rush gleefully towards death, but good spiritual training does prepare us for the inevitable.'

Various religions have different view on what happens after death. These are, generally, broken into three main styles.

Resurrectionalists

Some Christians believe that at the Last Judgement, the dead will literally return to life, body and soul rising from the grave, be transported to the Judgement then to heaven or hell for eternity. Until that day, the dead merely 'sleep'. Some variations say that the soul is in limbo until this date; others that the soul is judged soon after death and the reward of heaven or hell is virtually immediate.

Reincarnation

The soul of the dead will, at some point, be reborn in a new body to carry on its spiritual journey. Pythagorean reincarnation beliefs hold that human souls can only ever be reborn as humans – whereas some other religions believe that the soul can move through the various species of animals also.

Ancestral

Some religions do not have the concept of divine reward or punishment, simply that the spirit moves to live on in another plane or dimension. The newly dead join those who have gone before and, according to societal custom, are to be avoided or propitiated.

But what proof do we have that death is not the end? Spiritism believes that the dead go rattling around in the halls of eternity, popping back every now and then to check up on those left behind. There's regression that will find some interesting previous life for us to have inhabited. And last but not least, we have pre- or near-death precognition where the about-to-be-dead appear to someone miles away at the exact time they expired.

Love, Light and the Elements

The nearest thing to 'proof' is the consistent medical reports of 'near death experiences' which often occur during or after surgery. These reports are identical in that the patient floats through a long tunnel towards a brilliant light. Sometimes a figure appears to bar their entry, returning them to their earthly body and they survive to tell the tale. The figure is variously described as Jesus, an angel or a deceased member of the family. These near-death experiences give a tremendous amount of comfort to the recipient – but there is another side to consider.

There have also been reports of near-death experiences which take the patient down into darkness but these are infrequently mentioned for fear of causing alarm. Imagine sinking into the abyss, falling into bottomless darkness and then being revived . . . death would still hold all the terrors and none of the comforts for this recipient who would assume that they were headed straight for hell. Others report seeing flames or experiencing a floating sensation as though suspended in water.

On a spiritual level we can dispense with the equation of light = good; darkness = evil because these are arbitrary concepts not spiritual ones. Anyone who has even a passing interest in astrology will be familiar with the elemental groupings of earth, air, fire and water that in esoteric terms align with the four cardinal points of the compass. The 12 signs of the zodiac also fall into Earth signs (Taurus, Virgo, Capricorn), Air signs (Gemini, Libra, Aquarius), Fire signs (Aries, Leo, Sagittarius) and Water signs (Cancer, Scorpio, Pisces), all of which are supposed to govern the way we think and react according to when and where we were born.

The belief that the stars and planets – or cosmic influences – rule our lives is a very ancient one dating back to the priesthoods of Chaldea and Babylon. Like all archaic sciences, however, it became trivialised as the ancient wisdom was submerged under modernisation. The grains of information were recorded for posterity but not the interpretation or understanding. If humans are made up of these basic elements then perhaps that's what we return to at death, before we re-emerge in another incarnation. For those whose element is Air *will* be drawn to the light, while those of the Earth will be drawn back into the bosom of the Earth. Fire doesn't represent the flames of hell but cosmic fire. Water suggests the primordial waters from which everything originated

If you think this idea is far-fetched, just take a look at your own horoscope and see if it doesn't answer a few of those anomalies, or do you find that you're often at odds with your birth sign? Is your compatible partner the one listed by the astrologers or not? This is only another theory, of course, but it does explain some of those awkward questions that always crop up when we're thinking about life, death and the universe. If you think that it's all nonsense, just file this idea away and we'll return to it later in the book with other evidence to support the theory.

Listening to God's Heartbeat

Unfortunately the term 'shamanism' is another of those ancient concepts that has been debased through modern usage. Everyone wants to be a shaman these days, complete with that infernal drumming that drives everyone round the bend. Add misrepresentation in the media and we're ready to dismiss the whole idea as more New Age twaddle. The actual word comes from Siberia but it's now used as an umbrella for anything that smacks of indigenous tribal ritual workings.

> Traditionally the shaman, or medicine man, was the tribal mediator between God and the people. He walked the spirit path and accompanied souls on their final journey.

Esoteric writer Billie Walker-John raised the question of genuine traditional shamanic abilities when writing about the early priesthood of ancient Egypt which may offer yet another 'proof' for life after death even in this day of hi-tech innovation. In comparing the subject matter of prehistoric cave paintings in the Caverne des Tois Frères and the Fourneau de Diable in France with inscriptions found in Egypt, Billie Walker-John describes the function of the pre-dynastic shaman, although the Egyptians did not use the word to describe this priestly being – he was known there as the Sem-priest:

'The greatest part of this primordial knowledge had to do with the equally primordial Egyptian belief in the life after death. The Sem knew that the intangible psycho-spiritual elements – the soul, the double, the shining spirit, the name, the spiritual heart – of each person survived death because he had himself experienced its mysteries and survived them via his shamanic abilities. The rulers of the Pharaonic State were fully conscious of the Sem's use in ensuring their own Otherworldly immortality, and made full use of this ability.'

This belief endured for over 4,000 years and although all the old wisdom was swept away in the cultural and social upheaval at the end of the Pyramid Age, comparable fragments of an identical shamanic nature can be found on every continent. Regardless of what the shaman was called in his own people's language, an integral part of his training was to literally die and come back to life again in order to demonstrate his ability to pass into the Otherworld and return again. Only then was he deemed fit to accompany the souls of his tribe into the spirit realms.

There are people alive today who can perform this service but you won't find any of them banging drums on pagan camp sites. The regular, rhythmic drumming which sends the authentic shaman into his trance-like state could quite easily be thought of as the very heartbeat of his God.

Bridging the Divide

Bridging the divide between new ideas and religious teaching will always create its own set of problems. The deeper our level of understanding, the more waspish our priest is likely to be when it comes to matters of theology. As the Bishop of Edinburgh pointed out: 'Priesthoods, sacred or secular . . . create a place of power for themselves by getting into a position between nature and God, or humanity and political ideology.'

For hundreds of years priests have been accepted as God's chosen mediators of value and truth, and any form of disobedience of the religious law was instantly labelled 'sin'. To compound this power, the only method by which man could reconcile himself with God was to allow the priest to intercede on his behalf. This in turn established the priest in the mediating role of fixer or broker. 'This was one of the assumptions that Jesus, speaking from within the prophetic tradition, challenged by his claim that the kingdom of God was brokerless; it required no mediator, so that people did not have to be issued passports by the priesthood to achieve access to God,' concluded the Bishop.

There are duties that require the services of a priest and, just as you wouldn't consider removing your own appendix, certain rites of passage remain the province of the priesthood. When it comes to spiritual development, however, we can often find the machinations of the priesthood more of a hindrance than a help. This *impasse* is often because the priest is unable to understand where you're coming from with your new line of questioning – and you're unable to explain since you're none to clear about what it is you're seeking. All s/he can see is a lamb straying from the fold, while all you perceive is a blank wall of non-cooperation.

As Karen Armstrong rightly points out, we cannot easily understand the old forms of spirituality for it is no longer possible to follow a religious path in the same way as our ancestors did. We cannot bridge the divide by cobbling together an eclectic mish-mash of different cultures and label it a religion. Neither can we revive old cultures by dragging them kicking and screaming into the twenty-first century while parading about in fancy robes and adopting ridiculous names.

Unless we wish to become enmeshed in the spiritual void that threatens to engulf modern culture, we bridge the divide by serious study and practice. All the candle burning, meditation, drumming and chanting in the world will not compensate for a lack of direction. It must be acknowledged, of course, that many people feel liberated by a loss of faith because there are no longer any restrictions on the way they live their lives. This liberation often manifests in the popular pick and mix neo-paganism that happily mixes all the deities in a gigantic free-for-all.

Despite this apparent loss or abandonment of faith, many people still want to be religious, and new paths and traditions spring up all over the place, trying to attract new adherents. Frequently we find groups going into schism simply because they cannot speak the same language, or see things from another's point of view. 'What seems sacred and positive in one camp appears demonic and deranged in another,' comments Karen Armstrong.

Try it now	Taking your own needs into account, do you feel that your spiritual path should offer: ◆ Something stimulating or challenging? ◆ Something less demanding? ◆ Something new and/or exciting?

There's an old Zen saying that to walk the path is to *become* the path. By this stage on our journey we realise that we cannot actively quest for our spiritual identity by reading books and remaining casual observers. The time for play-acting is over and we must seriously accept that unless we allow that divine spark to ignite our soul (psyche, or inner self), then we will remain spiritual tourists, only there for the entertainment value. The time has come for assuming responsibility for our future actions.

The Burden of Enlightenment

The term enlightenment has been bandied around for many years now, to such a degree that it has almost become meaningless in the West. Nevertheless enlightenment is what *we* are seeking. Throughout the book we've talked of discipline but when it comes to enlightenment we cannot control the circumstances under which we receive it because it is not something we can create for ourselves. Discipline allows us to control the effect and after-math of the experience – not the experience itself.

Neither would we be wise to count one blinding flash of inspiration or guidance as enlightenment. Here, Zen offers a good example of what we should look for when it comes to understanding the differences in the variety of experience that come our way when we begin to tread the spiritual path. We should never fool ourselves that we've had a full mind-blowing experience when, in fact, we've only registered one on the Richter scale.

Satori is the term used to describe a state of consciousness beyond the plane of discrimination and differentiation. It means 'the first showing'. This experience may vary in quality and duration from a flash of intuitive awareness to Nirvana (the limitations of existence). It is the *beginning* and not the true end of spiritual development; it may be far removed from enlightenment in terms of long years of training. *Kensho*, which means 'seeing into one's own nature', is the goal of Zen practice and the first experience of *satori*. Therefore we will undergo a series of mini-enlightenments before we hit the big time; and even then we've still got a long way to go.

Whatever it is that we experience, however, must be put into perspective. Unless we have put our hearts and minds in order and asked ourselves all the pertinent questions in coming to terms with our individual weaknesses, we cannot expect success. The following are traditional qualities expected in a student of Zen but they are equally applicable for every other path. You must:

◆ Want to attain 'it', whatever you perceive 'it' to be.
◆ Possess humility that is consistent with a will to succeed.
◆ Accept that faith will be tested over and over again.
◆ Have a mind of your own and a measure of control over it.
◆ Be profoundly aware of the limits of the intellect.
◆ Possess a well balanced mind that will not buckle under the strain.
◆ Have an innate feeling for the path you have chosen.

Accounts of how the experience manifests can be found in religious and mystical literature from every faith but it can best be likened to the more familiar 'state of grace'. The fleeting moment, whilst leaving us momentarily dazed and exhilarated, creates a craving for more experiences of a similar nature.

Beware of False Prophets

It is often when we are in this state of spiritual limbo that we can fall prey to unscrupulous gurus who hover on the periphery of the seeker's vision, whispering from the shadows. Because we become desperate for more mystical experiences it is easy to become tempted by those who claim to be able to help us along the path – if only we'll just step down this side road. More often than not the diversion ends in tears and recriminations because at this stage of our journey we are more vulnerable than ever. We *want* to believe; we *want* to experience – and we're willing to follow anyone who promises to show us the way. At this point many a seeker becomes lost in a series of one-way systems and blind alleys to such a degree that they either settle for second best or give up the quest altogether. This is where we find our fellow travellers fall into several different categories.

- Those who are looking for a guru who will tell them what to do. Often they tarry a while hoping to find what they haven't been able to with other teachers.
- Those who seize upon anything that's new in order to be different amongst their own social set. They play for a while and then follow the next new fad because they don't want to put in the hard work necessary for a true spiritual quest.
- Those who are desperately seeking that unidentifiable *something* to fill a void in their lives. Often they're looking for a new set of rules to apply to their daily routine and will experiment with other cultures that appear attractive to them.
- Those who will embrace the system on a physical or superficial level. They want the recognition and rank without putting in the effort to acquire genuine knowledge.
- Those who from the very first introduction know that this is what they've always wanted. This is what they *are*. They no longer need to follow the path, the path has found them. They have become the path.

At present there's a great deal of nonsense being talked about teachers and students, and about the inheritance of teaching by favoured pupils, entitling them to pass the truth on to their own adherents. According to the translation of *The Collection of Stone and Sand* traditionally, there is only one way knowledge should be imparted: from heart to heart. 'Silence and humility reigned rather than profession and assertion. The one who received such teaching kept the matter hidden even after 20 years. Not until another discovered through his own need that a *real* master was at hand was it learned that the teaching had been imparted, and even then the occasion arose quite naturally and the teaching made its way in its own right. Under no circumstances did the teacher ever claim "I am the successor of So-and-so." 'Such a claim would prove quite the contrary.'

Although written at the turn of the century the message still holds true and today's seeker must be even more sceptical when presented with an impressive set of credentials. Despite the desire to pursue a spiritual quest, the seeker will find that it is often necessary to teach themselves by reading, studying and meditating on basic principles. There is an ancient Buddhist statement: 'When the pupil is ready, the Master appears.' This implies that the student must advance by his or her own efforts before they need or have 'earned' the physical presence of a teacher – in whatever guise they appear.

The Personal Universe

Any classical painting is executed according to the laws of perspective. What this means is that the items which the artist has painted smaller, the viewer feels are further away; items painted larger appear to be nearer. The artist can also make you feel that you are floating up in the air looking down on a subject; or in a valley looking upwards; or in any direction *he* chooses. The artist has chosen the direction from which you will view the subject, forcing you to look with his eyes – from his perspective.

This, however, is the only time you will ever view any part of the universe from anyone else's perspective because the whole of the universe can only be seen by you, from wherever *you* happen to be.

> There is an old Celtic riddle which asks: 'Where is the centre of the universe?' and the answer is always 'Here!'

Everything we observe is seen from our own personal viewpoint – and we are not just talking about the way we use our eyes. We put our personal slant on everything we observe or experience; we all react differently and interpret the world around us from differing viewpoints.

From the moment we are born, however, we are trained to interpret the world in a certain way. These lessons condition us so that we know how to communicate with those around us and give mutual reference points on how to behave within our own particular group or culture. When we begin to move into different realms of thought, these mutual signposts get fewer and further between. The meanings become more fluid, more open to interpretation. This is especially so when we come into areas concerned with personal beliefs. This is where the feeling that one is isolated in a strange personal universe can become too much for some folks; they feel safer with the herd, where the signs are more clear-cut and tangible.

When we start to think about personal spirituality, or spiritual development, the signposts become even more 'iffy' and those who try to help can often only give you hints and tips on finding your own way. This may give the appearance of being evasive but in reality they are simply confirming that no one *but you* can interpret your personal universe.

Signposts and Milestones

We have to accept that there is no one way by which we can achieve spiritual enlightenment; even the most experienced teacher can only point a student in the right direction. Here we also have to accept that there are two clear stages of spiritual development:

◆ our own journey to the gateway of our true path
◆ and the travelling along the path itself.

Many seekers find it difficult to accept that it may be a long road before they reach the entrance. In mystical terms this is the 'gate of conversion' – the spiritual point of no return. Before we reach this point we must learn how to know ourselves. This is where the understanding of the *kensho* and *satori* experiences enable the seeker to see how far they have travelled and not fool themselves into believing that they have arrived.

A Zen teacher describes this stage of the journey as the seeker stumbling blindly through the gloom of his or her own ignorance (and inexperience) to find the gate. 'Initiation into the mysteries of the way needs no divine initiator save as we choose to project that concept out of the human mind,' he wrote. 'We test ourselves, or are tested by our own past karma; we succeed in or we fail that test – and it may be that we shall fail it again and again. Then suddenly . . . we are on the way, and thereafter there is but one command, walk on! – and one obedience.'

We need to make sure that we've left all our 'baggage' at base camp since it will only hamper our upward climb. This does not mean discarding or rejecting our former beliefs, but retaining the understanding of our own culture so that we are not unconsciously influenced by the past. Coming to terms with what we are leaving behind means that we can take it or leave it without fear, guilt or a sense of rebellion.

It is extremely difficult for those grappling with the influences of monotheism to discard the god-concept of reward and punishment. We often find it hard to accept situations which we personally do not approve or fully understand, holding firmly on to the belief that there are predetermined ways of doing things. In the Buddhist holy book, *The Voice of Silence*, we find the words: 'The path is one for all; the means to reach the goal must vary with the pilgrim.' We must continue to examine our own personal reason for this spiritual quest.

Listen to the Stones Growing

Meditation and reflection are an important part of spiritual development. In the East it has been traditionally used as a means to connect with the absolute, while in the West it has been the mystic's path to God. What we need to be able to do at this stage of our journey is to gradually introduce a period of reflection on a daily basis. Why? Because spiritual development, when undertaken seriously, becomes a way of living; it is not a hobby, social activity or part time learning.

The quest will be unceasing and the first experiences will, more often than not, be unpleasant on whichever path we tread. We must get to grips with this realisation so that there are no nasty surprises to be discovered later on. We will find ourselves stepping from a well-worn path into a fog which conceals quick sands, sheer rock and apparently inhospitable wilderness. We must learn to walk on and observe what was previously hidden. Though we may receive a map and encouragement from a teacher, we must walk on alone.

We need to understand why we are pursing this intangible 'something'. In *The Road Less Travelled*, Dr M. Scott Peck defines it as a 'powerful force originating outside of human consciousness which nurtures the spiritual growth of human beings.' But however we attempt to explain or define it – either in religious or scientific terms – we cannot ignore its existence. This power or force exists and it is very, *very* real.

Spiritual development is something that happens to an individual when scales begin to fall from the eyes and the world is perceived in a different light. It doesn't matter whether we are male or female, young or old, there is no restriction on our perception because the 'something' is neither ageist nor sexist. No matter in which way we decide to express this pursuit of the inconceivable we have to accept responsibility for our own actions and the repercussions.

Try it now   Record the answers to the following in your journal:
- ◆ What does spiritual growth mean to you?
- ◆ Does it offer a sense of inner peace and harmony?
- ◆ Can you feel a sense of the Divine in the world around you?

It may be too soon to answer the questions above simply because it means *thinking* about them. In terms of spiritual growth, the intellect can often stifle the natural flow of reflection and /or inner peace. Many highly respected mystics have been simple folk, whose minds were not hindered by the demands of commerce or intellect.

Case Study_____

Tom's family was Catholic and for him to marry it was necessary for his fiancée to convert to Catholicism. When the local incumbent of the Anglican church retired, the village was assigned a young vicar, Mr Strong, in whom 'the Spirit burned brightly'. Not because he was a fanatic, or rammed his message down everyone's throat but because he was a genuinely nice, hard-working man with a family, who took his duties as a parish priest seriously. Whereas his predecessor had spent most of his time propping up the bar in the local pub, the new vicar visited people in the village.

Although Tom's family was Catholic Mr Strong visited the house, talking for hours on end. The vicarage became a centre for village activities, with parties and fetes in the garden, concerts in the long lounge with its piano. Choir practices were held there, as were confirmation classes. The congregation grew from less than a dozen to over 60 on a regular basis. Tom's family was included and Tom himself started to help the vicar; he'd been an altar boy at the Catholic church when he was young, and became an altar server.

Because Tom was Catholic he had to meet with the Bishop of the Diocese to get a special dispensation for him to serve in the church and also to become a lay preacher. The vicar introduced Tom to some of the more obscure church rituals, including ,holding vigils in the church. Despite reviving attendances in a declining rural area, the vicar was not popular with the church hierarchy. He was too different, too charismatic – too alternative. Not only did he like incense and 'strange' services but he also had the unfortunate habit of healing people by laying on of hands.

Eventually the vicar was manoeuvred into a political corner and forced to resign. The next one had worked in Africa for far too long, and believed the villagers should hold him in awe as his position demanded; the church attendance declined and Tom's enthusiasm waned. He'd been drawn to a genuine priest who was an extraordinary man: 'There was certainly something about him as he preached,' he recalls. 'I can remember watching him as he stood black against the cream-washed walls of the church, and you could see around him that aura of fire which is depicted in religious paintings. But he was never ever arrogant, or pushy, and would make jokes about himself. I believe he was a true man of God.

'As vicars in the surrounding parishes retired or moved away, rather than replacing them the Diocese lumped their pastoring needs onto him. He would rotate the services so that each village got a turn to have Eucharist once a month, and we all got used to motoring from church to church. We made friends with folks in other village churches and we would all rotate from church to church with the congregation growing as more and more got involved. Things were never the same when he left.' _____

Summary

A spiritual quest will often challenge many of your preconceived ideas about what you want to explore. We can often find ourselves changing direction unconsciously or unintentionally, as personal values come under the microscope and we are forced to re-examine the rules which have governed our lives.

     ◆ Which personal values does your spiritual quest challenge?
     ◆ Are you prepared to meet those challenges?
     ◆ Do you want to continue your quest, or remain a bystander?

There should be no sense of failure should you choose not to continue. Even if you feel that an advanced spiritual approach to life is not for you, perhaps your perceptions have expanded a little to allow you to look on others with more understanding. If this is the case, then you have not failed in your intent.

A spiritual
quest is
discovering the
most direct
experience of
God.

CHAPTER 9

Finding the Answers

O f the Four Noble Truths in the Buddhist canon the first is:
Life is suffering. Life is a series of difficulties and problems
but if we can accept this as a *fact* of life, then we can cope with
adversity and rise above it. Most people find it extremely difficult
to accept this philosophy, however, and prefer to bemoan their lot.
They take the stance that life should be fair and that it has singled
them out for the messy end of the stick.

'Finding a new belief isn't going to reverse the stick,' comments
Mel, our spiritual mentor. 'The only thing that will make
problems go away is dealing with them and instilling a sense of
discipline into the daily routine. Of course, it can be painful, but
it's not possible to attempt any form of spiritual growth while
you're hauling a lot of baggage around. I find that people still
retain a subconscious need for a saviour of some kind, even
working on the principle of: "If I follow this god s/he will be so
grateful, they'll grant my request".'

Setting out on a spiritual journey has its own attendant
problems that will only be exacerbated by clinging on to old
problems and difficulties. We need a clear head and a clear eye to
be able to discern which teaching will help us on our way, and
which will muddy the waters. We are looking for sensible
information to absorb during our travels. Unfortunately, many of
the books that purport to give the answers to spiritual dilemma
add further confusion by not offering sound, *practical* advice on
how to set about accomplishing your goal.

The Spiritual Onion

At the beginning of this book we explained that religion and
spirituality are not the same thing. They may run parallel to each
other, at times the line may even merge, but they remain separate.
A good analogy might be to use the layers of an onion to describe
where religion leaves off and spirituality takes over.

The outer skin of the onion represents the fundamental religious doctrine, a skilful blend of myth and fable by which the teaching is conveyed to members of the congregation from an early age. These stories refer to the origins of a particular culture and provide a meaning for the trials and tribulations of day-to-day living. The language is simplistic and used to create a framework on which that society hangs, with the priesthood's guiding hand on the tiller.

The next layer caters for those of a higher intellect or social position, who cannot be held in check by simple stories. They need to question and require sensible, informed answers if their support for the religion is to continue. The religion is sustained by introducing a greater sense of personal or group involvement. As the layers are stripped away the emphasis leans more heavily on spirituality. Two priests or monks and nuns discussing faith will converse on a different, more intimate level than the student-tutor lectures at theological college. As we get to the inner core of the onion we find that the layers are much smaller and thinner but it is from here that new growth will spring. Here the myths and fables take on the mystical elements that remain at the heart of every faith.

Learning through reading

When we start out on a spiritual quest we are reliant on the 'stories' available to the general reader. Keeping the onion analogy in mind may help you to sift through the hundreds of books on offer and discover those that speak to you direct. 'People are always willing to recommend books but I usually find that when I settle down for a good read I'm quickly bored by the superficial approach to the subject,' complained one student.

Decide what sort of reading material would appeal most to you:

◆ a reader-friendly primer that tells you it's all so easy
◆ a 'warts-and-all' study of the subject that doesn't pull its punches
◆ an academic thesis.

Reading is of course a matter of personal taste but a considerable amount of time can be wasted if the seeker gets bogged down with useless information. Learn to be more discerning about what

you read in books and don't labour under the misapprehension
that just because the book is in print the author understands what
they are talking about.

The 'Bread' We Live By

The true nature of a spiritual quest is to discover the most direct
experience of God and we generally refer to this as 'mysticism'. In
modern society the term is loosely and incorrectly used to
describe occult and paranormal phenomena such as divination,
telepathy and healing and it is well to understand this is what
mysticism is *not*. Although many genuine mystics possess such
powers, they are not essential to the mystical experience itself.
Neither should we believe that mysticism and the mystical
experience are universal since there are both important *and* subtle
differences between beliefs.

All religions have their mystics and priesthood, although the
priests greatly out-number the mystics, who tend to be very thin
on the ground. The priesthood has been described as 'those who
minister close to the altars of convention. They are the salesmen
of wares handed on to them and the distributors of tradition.
They do not so much create as conserve.' The mystic, on the other
hand, remains on the outer reaches of society, unhampered by the
customs and traditions of their own people. They follow wherever
their spiritual path takes them; their vision is open and far-
reaching.

Embracing mysticism

The priesthood is often extremely sceptical – even about the
mystical experiences of its own members. One of the problems to
an organised religion is that you cannot regulate who will have the
mystical or spiritual experience. The higher the title in the church,
temple, synagogue or mosque does not necessarily mean the
greater degree of spirituality. God forbid that an ordinary man or
woman should start to experience what a high priest or patriarch
does not!

By looking across the divide to other religions we learn to
believe in a 'worthy God'; a God of all peoples, whatever their
colour, race or creed. There's a Buddhist saying that there are as
many paths as there are men; a Hindu will tell you that truth

shines out more brilliantly when it shines from many angles. The non-proselytising religions will urge you *not* to give up your own religious heritage but to see it from a different perspective through the words of its great mystics rather than the dogmas of its priests.

According to the Law

It is grossly unfair to judge or condemn any religious belief by its quirks and foibles, simply because every religion has them tucked away in its teaching. If we take the Ten Commandments on which Christianity is based, we find that only two of these break temporal law and yet all ten in the eyes of the church would be considered 'mortal' sins, entailing loss of grace and damnation. Those that are popularly known as the Seven Deadly Sins are of a 'venial' nature and do not entail loss of all grace. Both forms of sin are forgiven if real regret and true resolve to lead a new life are sincerely expressed.

The Buddhist faith is governed by what is known as the Four Noble Truths and the Noble Eight-Fold path. The former are:
1. that existence is unhappiness
2. that unhappiness is caused by selfish desire or craving
3. that desire can be destroyed
4. that it can be destroyed by following the Noble Eight-Fold Path whose steps are:
   ◆ right view
   ◆ right desires
   ◆ right speech (plain and truthful)
   ◆ right conduct (including abstinence not only from immorality but also from taking life, whether human or animal)
   ◆ right livelihood (harming no one)
   ◆ right effort (always pressing on)
   ◆ right awareness (of the past, the present and the future)
   ◆ right contemplation of meditation.

Buddhism teaches the way of spiritual liberation through ethics and discipline. A universal God plays no part in this religion, and often no word exists for the concept that was neither affirmed nor denied by Buddha himself, but simply *ignored*. In the West we have a saying that a man reaps what he sows and Buddhists believe that character is made up of the thoughts and actions that a person has 'sown'. The effects of the thoughts and actions are what is reborn – not the 'inner self' or the soul.

By comparison Christianity may appear to be conducted on a bartering system, whereby the penitent confesses to the sin and, on promising not to do it again, receives forgiveness. Buddhists, on the other hand, must take responsibility for their own actions and be prepared to pay the price of any negative karma their thoughts or deeds attract. Look for the differences in the 'small print' – the *similarities* are much more obvious.

Try it now	How do you feel about studying the beliefs of other faiths? Do you regard them as: ◆ An object of curiosity? ◆ Less pure or genuine? ◆ A challenge to the intellect?

Most of us have been taught our religious beliefs and politics in the form of institutionalised instruction, and firmly believe in that body's interpretation of the 'facts'. Institutionalised religion is, by its very nature, divisive: it drives a wedge between believers (those of its own faith) and non-believers (those of all other faiths).

Mind, Body and Spirit

Take a look through any of the New Age magazines and you'll find a plethora of Eastern practices that have been absorbed into Western culture.

Hinduism

Most of this has its roots in Hinduism and its holy books *The Vedas*. On the surface this Indian religion has a colourful pantheon of gods and goddesses, images and idols, exotic temples and sacred palaces with their rituals and offerings. At its highest level (known as Brahmanism) however, the belief manifests in a subtle and sophisticated form of monotheism.

To quote a yoga teacher: 'Hinduism has always been mystical to its core, since it has always taught that by yogic techniques man can realise, here and now, the eternal and Divine within himself.

So imminent is the Deity that to claim to be God is quite natural since, in some sense, everything is God.'

Taoism

Taoism is one of the three great religions of China. It stems from a mere 5,000 characters on a bamboo parchment left by its founder Lao Tze when on his last journey to an unknown destination. The *Tao Te Ching* is one of the world's great religious classics that many adherents believe to enshrine the wisdom of the universe; the teachings are 'paradoxical, inverse, passive and irrational'.

Although *tao* means 'course' or 'way', Taoism does not point to any identifiable way and is described as having reality but no form, being impalpable, invisible and incapable of being expressed in words. It can, however, be achieved by virtue, by compassion, by humility and non-violence. 'There is no personal God and such Gods as men imagine are mere emanations of Tao which gives life to all things. Tao is Being.' Thus Tao is the source of all created things; existing before the universe it extends perfect balance and harmony through the release of its energy.

Confucianism

Much of the Chinese view of the universe, the Gods and human morality was based on the teachings of Confucius. While Taoism is essentially a mystical philosophy recommending doing nothing and resisting nothing, Confucianism is a practical code of living with its founder insisting on intervening in everything to do with social life. In order that people might know how to live, Confucius described the Superior Man with 'five constant virtues':

- ◆ *Right attitude* – the desire to be in harmony with others, an inner law of self-control.
- ◆ *Right procedure* – the study of the rules of conduct and knowing how to apply them in every incident.
- ◆ *Right knowledge* – receiving the education to respond in the correct way.
- ◆ *Right moral courage* – necessary to remain loyal to one's self and one's neighbours.
- ◆ *Right persistence* – The Superior Man has achieved the other four virtues, and he persists in his achievement. He is unfailingly kind and helpful. Because he has developed the

seeds of virtue within his nature, he is in harmony with the universe.

Shinto

Shinto, the indigenous religion of Japan, works quite successfully in tandem with Buddhism. Meaning 'the way of the Gods', the followers of Shinto see themselves as a small part of everything that exists – having an empathy with nature that the average Westerner struggles to regain, despite the growth of nature consciousness in the West. The Japanese believe that the same wonderful forces that move in nature, move in themselves; there is no dividing line between the human and the divine. Their natural surroundings speak of beauty and purity and are looked upon with reverence.

The God-shelf – the centre of Shinto worship in the home – does not contain images of their Gods (of which there are many), only an abstract symbol. On this shelf they place tablets or slips of paper on which are written the names of the Gods they are honouring. A light burns there, with daily prayers and offerings made by the family. Although Shinto embraces ancestor worship, it does not emphasise life beyond death; Buddhism has, however, filled this gap for the traditional Japanese.

The warring factions

Christian mysticism

Christian mysticism is rarely talked about at grass roots level (although there are numerous books available on the subject) and characteristically it is centred on prayer. Christians believe that when the human body dies its elements blend with the earth but the human soul is eternal. This human soul is closely linked to God, since God is the eternal spirit, existing from before creation. Christians believe that each soul is individual, having been united with an individual body since before the person's birth; through the union of soul and body a person is brought into being.

Most Christians insist that God's grace offers eternal life or some kind of heaven. One scholar commented that the intense concern that some folk have about the after life is not a sign of inner health and genuine faith in life's possibilities. 'Rather it reveals a lack of faith and confidence in life.'

There are numerous forms of Christian mysticism:

◆ The liturgical and sacramental which sees and uses the sacraments as means of ascent to God.

◆ Devotional mysticism centred on meditation on the person, life and teaching of Jesus. Many Franciscan writers favour this tradition.

◆ The contemplative tradition which takes different forms in Eastern (Hesychasm) and Western (Meister Eckhart) schools.

◆ Large family schools including the Carmelite, the Ignatian and Berulle, which use discursive meditation as a means of preparation in the earliest stages of the path, and then move to contemplative prayer.

Islam

Devout Muslims turn their faces to Mecca five times a day in a ritual of prayer laid down some 14 centuries ago by Mohammed and today Islam is one of the most widespread religions. Islam came later than the other two great monotheistic religions and Mohammed accepted much of the inspiration of the Old Testament. He claimed to be a successor of Moses and although he did not recognise Jesus as the Son of God, he accepted him as a prophet.

The *Koran*, next to the Bible, is the most influential book in the world and its ethical teachings are high. The great advantage of Islam is that, like Judaism, it is a literal-minded religion lived in every-day life and no Muslim is left in any doubt as to how to conduct themselves on a daily basis. Those believers who have followed the will of Allah will be eternally rewarded by residence in the garden of paradise; the more spiritually inclined believe paradise to be the eternal presence of Allah. For those who decline to submit to the will of Allah, a place in hell has been prepared.

Judaism

Judaism is perhaps the most fascinating of the 'big three' simply because it is the mother religion of both Christianity and Islam. From Judaism the other two faiths inherited most of their religious ideas, morals and practices. The basic creed of Judaism is based on the concept of a transcendent and omnipotent one true God; the revelation of His will in the Torah; and the special relationship between God and His 'chosen people'.

Judaism is essentially a social and family religion which, more than almost any other concerns itself with the observances of every aspect of daily life. As in Islam strict details are laid down for the behaviour of the orthodox, the home being the main 'institution' for the Jewish tradition where the woman's place is considered sacred.

The Tree of Life

The Qabalah (Hb. *Kabbalah* = that which is received) was originally a collection of Jewish doctrines about the nature of the universe, traditionally handed down by Moses to the Rabbis, which evolved into a mystical interpretation of the Old Testament. Strictly speaking it is a system of Jewish mystical thought which appears to have originated in southern France and Spain in the twelfth–thirteenth centuries. Qabalah was one of the many terms (true knowledge, inner knowledge, knowledge of the mysteries, hidden wisdom) used to designate this secret lore.

Christian interest in the tradition developed in the fifteenth century specifically attempting to prove that the doctrines about the nature of Christ were the true and secret meanings of the Jewish system. During the seventeenth century it took on the form of natural philosophy, alchemy and neo-Platonism and by the eighteenth century 'percolated into the symbolism of Freemasonry'. By the time it had passed through the nineteenth–twentieth centuries the Qabalah was associated with modern European occultism and ritual magic. In America it has become a 'religion' in its own right attracting more than its fair share of Hollywood celebrities.

The Qabalistic Tree of Life teaches how the creation of the universe took place through a series of emanations from the Godhead. These emanatory structures are represented by ten spheres or *sephiroth*, arranged across three columns. Each sphere can only be understood in relation to its neighbours, where it appears on the Tree and how it is affected by the descent of power from the Godhead. They represent a finely balanced harmony enabling the flow of divine energy to sustain man and nature.

The Qabalah is *not*, in itself, a religion but it can be viewed as a spiritual philosophy that transcends or complements a religious belief. One senior occultist recommended that everyone should create their own Tree of Life for the purpose of understanding Divine power on a cosmic scale.

Revivalists and Reconstructionalists

When it comes to the pagan beliefs such as Wicca, we find there is very little to offer in the way of formal spiritual exploration although the followers of this new religion pay homage to 'the Goddess' and her consort, the Horned God. Wicca is an eclectic blend of reconstructed European and Mediterranean folk-lore (which is best described as pantheistic) with a dash of Eastern promise. At the moment Wicca is too fragmented to have developed its own 'mysteries' simply because the majority of adherents work as individuals or with a partner, rather than as a group. The beliefs are predominately nature orientated and there is an active social calendar for the pagan scene.

Traditions such as Druidry, Asatru (Norse), Celtic, Egyptian and Tradition/Hereditary Craft tend to be much more formal and spread their teaching programmes over a five- to seven-year period. These groups draw on authentic sources and can be intense when it comes to their religious beliefs, which they take *very* seriously – especially members of the priesthood. The various Traditions and Orders amongst the revivalists groups are unlikely to be found performing publicly since they tend to be much more private than Wicca.

Try it now

Answer the following and record your responses in your journal:

◆ Of all the traditions mentioned in this chapter, which one would you like to know more about?

◆ And why?

◆ How is it different from your own belief?

◆ Are you interested in the other tradition because it is completely different from your own or do you feel comfortable with the similarity?

It may be, of course, that you're beginning to look at your own faith with new eyes, and feel that you can develop your spiritual growth without making any change.

The Dark Side of God

When people change from one religion or spiritual path to another, the darker elements of 'God' are conveniently overlooked in the process. We must, however, understand that God, irrespective of the religious belief, is not there as some kind of divine lottery, handing out bouquets and brickbats. As we discussed in the second chapter, the wounded soul often comes into being because someone decides that God hasn't come up to scratch in the benevolence stakes and, as a result, support has been withdrawn until He toes the line.

The concept of God as creator/destroyer is an extremely ancient one and those of us on a spiritual quest will quickly begin to realise that there isn't a controlling deity who can be appeased by mere prayer or offering. We come back to the first of the Four Noble Truths which opened this chapter and hopefully can get to grips with the idea that the 'bad' things that happen in Life are not dictated by the whim of a malevolent super-being.

The other form of 'darkness' is, of course, the concept of evil that is undoubtedly one of the most ticklish of all theological questions. The fundamental doctrine of many Christian sects is reliant on the belief and acceptance of evil in the form of 'the Devil' but is there really any such thing as the personification of evil? Perhaps the best answer is one from the Qabalah:

'Evil is simply misplaced force. It can be misplaced in time: like the violence that is acceptable in war, is unacceptable in peace. It can be misplaced in space: like a burning coal on the rug rather than the fireplace. Or it can be misplaced in proportion: like an excess of love can make us overly sentimental, or a lack of love can make us cruel and destructive. It is in things such as these that evil lies, not in a personal Devil who acts as an Adversary.'

Maintaining Faith in Doubt

Questions demand answers and sometimes the answer we receive only makes us even more insecure or frightened than ever. The more information we gain when we're exploring spirituality only goes to prove just how small and insignificant we really are in the universal scheme of things. We suddenly start to question our reasons for starting out on this ridiculous journey in the first place. Why couldn't we have stayed at home, safe and snug instead of clambering up treacherous mountain slopes in search of our God – whatever and whoever it may be?

First, we'd be extremely worried if you *weren't* asking these questions. You may be wondering whether you've got to decide if you want to follow any religion. Perhaps you have been pleasantly surprised to find some of the other religions very different from what you expected. You may be worried about following a belief that could cause you to be outcast by your own community. Conversely, you may even have felt more kindly disposed towards your own religion, or discovered some deeper insights that your own faith has overlooked. As a theologian commented: 'It's a comfortable feeling to believe that one's own culturally given religion is the best of all religions – at least for oneself.'

You need to be sure about what is right for you because faith is some unshakeable belief you have in something regardless of what others may think. As Chrissie explains: 'It's knowing that there would be a great gaping hole in your life if you did not follow that path; in my own case knowing that I had the *potential* to be a true Wiccan priestess. But only if you put your reading into practice and live your life as a Wiccan priestess can you claim to be what you purport to be. I know that it's a big step to take, and a scary step, too. But if you cannot do it, then you are *not* a true spiritual being, because you couldn't bear to ignore the magic it brings to your life.'

Others from different spiritual and cultural backgrounds have all said the same: 'We might as well stop breathing as stop being a . . . Druid . . . an Egyptian priestess . . . a shaman . . . a magister . . . a wise woman . . .'

Standing on the Roof of the World

So here we are . . . we're standing on the roof of the world and hopefully our view will be a clear one. From here we can see just how far we've travelled and appreciate just how steep that final climb turned out to be. But we've made it. Our perceptions may have altered – perhaps only slightly – but we've reached a new understanding about both our inner and outer selves.

We've all seen those clear, bright photographs of Everest expeditions and from where we stand we can visualise the panorama of endless blue sky, white glistening peaks and feel the pure air with every breath we take. We understand that by accident of birth each of us has been born into a culture with its own attendant faith, tradition and religion. Long before we are considered to have reached maturity when we are free to make our own choices, most of us have become so thoroughly conditioned with 'culturally engendered values' that few ever take the radical steps to break free from family background and religion. On the other hand there will always be the few who need to discover for themselves the thrill and freedom of exploring those unknown spiritual pathways.

Case Study

'From childhood I'd always believed in some invisible "force" far greater than myself and learned that the label for this supernatural power was God,' recalls Angela. 'By my early teens I began to search this God out, attending the churches of several different denominations. At the same time I began collecting occult magazines. My interest was thwarted when my frantic mother banned the magazines as "unhealthy" and also my church attendances as she feared I was becoming a religious maniac.'

Following her grandmother's death when Angela was in her late twenties, she began her search again as she was desperate to find some form of faith that felt 'true' to her. She began Bible study that subsequently led to her becoming a Jehovah's Witness and such was her zeal that she underwent heart by-pass surgery without blood or blood-products. Even so, the more she learned, the more she questioned. She had also begun to be increasingly aware of an energy flow around herself that gave her a wonderful feeling of 'oneness' with the universe. Believing it to be the product of God's holy spirit, she wanted to share her experiences with others.

'To my confusion, others of my faith were puzzled and clueless . . . they obviously had never experienced these sensations. I also noticed that by "tuning in" to this energy whilst at prayer, I was answered in the most unbelievable ways. My husband at the time (now my ex-) was increasingly furious at his loss of control over me, as I was now expressing different views on life and so he declared an all-out open war upon me, using both physical and mental violence. He also used scare tactics by performing a type of exorcism on the living room carpet – anything to kill my joy of life. Eventually, I fled.'

Whilst staying with friends in Holland, Angela's experiences led her to reconsider Wicca. 'I was happy to discover a Goddess rather than just an unbalanced view of Godhead. Craft is for me a celebration of life – balanced and harmonious with Nature . . . I embraced the Horned God, the fertilising spirit of Nature, which is much more innocent than a God who represses his subjects with feelings of guilt concerning natural bodily functions. I believe in reincarnation and I suppose the Craft has been with me since well before my birth in this life . . . but it's taken 37 years to re-awaken.' _____

Summary

It is vital that we keep alive the need to search and question and not become complacent. The journey has not been without its blind alleys and dangers. But having travelled this far we now need to ask ourselves how satisfied we are with our progress.

- ◆ Are we content to have travelled this far and no further?
- ◆ Or are we to push on to the very end of our quest – wherever that may lead?

As our theologian pointed out: 'There is more faith in honest doubt than in all the unexamined creeds of the past and present.' It is only when we plumb the depths of personal experience that we can fully appreciate that all beliefs are very much alike – even though each individual following it is an original seeker.

CHAPTER 10

Rebuilding Faith in the Future

Having almost reached the end of our journey, we hope that you have started to put into motion a series of changes that will bring about the spiritual knowledge that you seek. As we've learned, there is always room for another idea, another explanation, an exchange of viewpoint, which enables us to celebrate our spiritual differences. It would be an extremely boring world if we were all the same. As the Dalai Lama observes, diversity means that we have different frameworks within which to 'locate ethical discipline and the development of spiritual values. That is why I do not advocate a new "world" or a "super" religion. It would mean that we would lose the unique characteristics of the different faith traditions.'

Self-Understanding and Self-Esteem

Unless the spiritual changes we hope to bring about are spontaneous and automatically become part of our daily life, then the transformation is incomplete. Going through the motions is not enough since this merely results in self-importance rather than self-esteem; by gaining self-understanding we inspire confidence within ourselves.

Returning to Dr Howard Cutler, we are told that a healthy sense of self-confidence is a critical factor in achieving our goals, that low self-confidence will inhibit our efforts 'to move ahead, to meet challenges, and even take some risks when necessary in the pursuit of our objectives.' On the other hand inflated self-confidence can be equally damaging and is a common condition that infects hundreds of so-called teachers of spirituality. This should set the alarm bells ringing in the mind of the seeker.

Dr Cutler describes those who suffer from an exaggerated sense of their own importance as being subject to 'frustration, disappointment and rage when reality intrudes and the world doesn't validate their idealised view of themselves' or they fail to live up to their own projected self-image. In addition, this grandiosity usually results in a kind of self-imposed arrogance that distances them from other people.

> Above all, to thine own self be true.

By adopting an inner honesty about yourself and your own abilities you will discover that honest self-appraisal can be a powerful weapon against self-doubt and low self-esteem.

Ex-nun Karen Armstrong suggests that the heavy demands that modern culture places on human beings, while broadening our horizons can also dent our confidence and self-esteem. We no longer understand where we are in the scheme of things. We are so concerned with building a 'life space' around ourselves that we may be unconsciously settling for a small, restricting place in life rather than stepping out into space.

Life really does appear to offer its richest rewards (not always in financial terms) to those who have developed the capacity to expand their 'life spaces'. While we would be unwise to believe we have *total* control over our surroundings, each of us does create a personal environment of attitudes and emotions which have a significant impact on our surroundings and the people with whom we come in contact.

Try it now | Have your attitudes towards other people changed since starting your quest? Do you find yourself:
- More willing to listen to others?
- Able to cope with demands made by other people?
- Less likely to get heated up about unimportant matters?

Building up self-esteem can influence the quality of your own life space and, as with the domino effect, can improve the quality of others'. This doesn't mean you should suffer fools gladly or bow to unreasonable demands on your time and space, but it does mean that you can extract yourself more easily without giving offence or causing hurt.

A Case for Humility

In the long-term this open-mindedness will probably not involve a change in our spiritual affiliations. It is quite possible that we can learn just as much about the importance of self-knowledge through a deeper study of our own faith as through the study of another religion. By re-examining our own faith we may discover that we have really experienced a widening of horizons and an extension of self-knowledge. We may also have gained in the process a deeper appreciation for our own religious tradition.

We often limit ourselves to what others tell us instead of re-examining the basic questions for ourselves. We cling to the beliefs emphasised by pre-adolescent schooling without taking the time to explore different avenues for ourselves. The more we explore and challenge the right of those beliefs to keep us in the dark about the positive aspects of other faiths, the greater our own concepts of the Divine.

With these new insights comes humility, the realisation that although we are but very small cogs in the gigantic system of things, we are an integral part of this enormous whole.

Redefining Your Goal

The path of true spirituality is made up from many different facets of light and shadow. As we have seen it begins with an understanding that all paths and journeys are valid on a spiritual quest, and a growing discernment over what are the *real* priorities in our lives. To bring about these changes of perception we need to develop an inner discipline and awareness of what we are and where we think we want to go. It may be thought strange to redefine spiritual goals at this late stage in the book but for the genuine seeker, any time is right. No boundaries have been crossed that cannot be retraced. Fear, guilt or uncertainty can have a blinkering effect on the seeker's mind – by looking neither left nor right it is easy to convince ourselves that this is the only way forward.

Try it now

Try to give honest, soul-searching answers to the following:

◆ What is it you want? Do you know? What do you believe your goal to be? Is the search of use if you don't know what you're looking for?

◆ Why do you want it? Motive becomes of increasing importance as the seeker climbs higher towards his or her goal.

- How much do you want it? Are you willing to pay the price, whatever it may be?
- Who wants it? You may claim that *you* do, but who or what are you? What part of you will gain from this quest?
- Where are you looking for it? Most seekers will respond 'within' but are we really searching our inner selves or do we still harbour some hope that an outside influence (god, teacher or book) will save us the trouble of long years of study and seeking?
- Have you the courage to find it? A spiritual quest often leads us into confrontation with our worst nightmares – do we have the will-power and endurance to endure the unpleasant and the terrifying along with the ecstatic and transcending?
- Are you fit for the rest of the journey? Can you cope with everything that will test your fitness to proceed and are you prepared to try again if the first attempts fail?

This approach to spiritual development rules out an uncritical reliance on other peoples' experiences. We have also drawn a line through beliefs that build walls around themselves, shutting out honest debate about why other people believe what they do.

Finding the Strength to Dream

According to psychologist Anny Wyse, grown-ups largely become grown-up by making mental, thinking decisions on what is 'real'. They discard great swathes of the universe because it doesn't fit into the tiny thinking-box that is their current mind. The Australian native people say that only so much of this world as we can dream of exists. The world gets bigger and more inclusive because we are able to dream greater dreams. Nelson Mandela said something similar.

'Modern scientific method tends to be that you have a hypothesis and then go looking for the evidence to support it,' explained Anny. 'Just so have people found quarks, DNA, new stars, viruses and, most recently, the shadow of a planet on its own sun nearer to us than the planet Mercury!

'I was trained in transpersonal psychology by two of the founders of this perspective in Britain. They had few limits on their thinking, an intelligent openness to new (to them) ways of working, and both had a deep spiritual practice which was part of their everyday being. I was fortunate – you don't get many psychologists of their calibre to the pound! Amongst psychologists outside their immediate sphere, however, I still had to fight for the right to be a shaman.

'Everyone, everything is capable of magic,' affirms Anny. 'Like driving a car, it takes practice and you have to learn the Highway Code. When the mind starts reaching beyond the current "known" the psyche is activated and can begin to spin threads outwards from the self to other parts of "otherworld". I live my life as a shaman. My pantheon is largely the Celtic one but by no means exclusively. I find the substance of the Gods is similar wherever one is in space and time, but the forms the Gods choose to wear changes as the land changes and the positions of the stars change as they move through time.

'The level on which these things (beings, images) become real is the place where we can leap beyond the fences and hedges and prison bars of "normal". Otherworld is real all the time and everywhere but we have to take our distorting and reducing lenses off in order to see it. And it has nothing to do with belief – although belief can be a first stepping stone to knowing. As Jung said: "I don't believe! I know!" And so do all mystics. Psychologists can often have serious difficulties with this as it seems not too many of them have a real concept of knowing, although they are very good at knowledge – not the same thing at all.

'Now – *arche* and *typos*, two Greek words put together to try to give imaginable shape and form to Gods. For many, to use the word archetype gives a respectable protection from those enormous concepts, like standing behind the safety fence at a firework display. If one uses the word 'God' it can become frighteningly up-close and personal. For the Gods are real and exist outside of, beyond and despite us. Perhaps this is some of the difficulty. If we have Gods then we may find ourselves insignificantly small in the great scheme of things. Most people don't have a sufficiently integrated and secure ego to be able to accept this with equanimity.

'But the gods are there. Otherworld is there. And here.'

The Otherworld Experience

The term 'otherworld' can have alarming connotations to those unfamiliar with the concept. We are not talking about 'ghoulies and ghosties, and long-legged beasties, and things that go bump in the night'. We're talking about those inexplicable *natural* occurrences such as dreaming, coincidences and *déjà vu* which we've all experienced. Who hasn't found themselves confused, intrigued or disconcerted by any of these happenings – or the involuntary shiver when 'someone walks over your grave'? We ponder and reflect for a moment and then forget about it until the next time.

Many things happen on the periphery of our 'vision' – occurrences that are so fleeting that it's only with hindsight, or when someone else talks about a similar experience, that we remember them. Under normal circumstances the lack of an acceptable explanation or interpretation discourages us from exploring further even if it leaves a residue of puzzlement in our mind. Those on a spiritual quest may find that these 'gateways between the worlds' or different levels of consciousness make them more aware of the open channel between these strange experiences.

If we talk of something as being 'other worldly' we are referring to those ethereal qualities summed up by the dictionary definition as: 'resembling celestial ether, light, airy, tenuous, subtle, exquisite, impalpable, spiritual'. We can often catch these sensations at dawn and dusk when natural light takes on an 'other worldly' quality, casting a translucent sheen over the landscape. If we stop and enjoy the moment, we're left with a feeling of exhilaration and vitality that can take several hours to evaporate and then we wonder why we allowed ourselves to be so moved by a normal occurrence. Then the moment is gone – until next time when we connect with our environment for a few precious moments.

Cosmic Consciousness

Once developed, the spiritual side of our nature enables us to interact with life on a cosmic scale, not merely confining ourselves to the mundane world. This may appear to smack of grandiose platitudes but this is what is meant by the terms 'microcosm' and 'macrocosm' which are bandied about in many New Age texts.

This theory illustrates the tendency of humankind to picture both Gods, and the surrounding landscape, in its own image. The universe is regarded as a human organism on a gigantic scale and mankind as a miniature copy. Although esoteric thinkers of the Renaissance adopted this theory, it was well known in medieval Europe, which in turn had inherited it from the Classical world, where again the universe was considered a living and divine organism.

Currently no longer regarded as having any scientific value, the theory has retained immense significance for present-day esoteric thinking, satisfying two powerful opposite feelings that humankind has about itself and its place in the universal scheme of things. These ideas are also illustrated by the Qabalah (whether in its context of Jewish or Christian mysticism), reflecting the relationship between humanity and the universe, while encouraging correspondences between the differing forces in the universe and their equivalent in man.

Such flashes of insight are not so rare as people would like to believe. Although not necessarily associated with specific religious traditions, examples occur in the mystical traditions of many cultures, including Christianity and Islam. A Canadian doctor, R. W. Bucke, coined the phrase 'cosmic consciousness' at the beginning of the twentieth century to describe the sensation of one's everyday personality dissolving and merging into the 'all'. Freud called it the 'oceanic feeling' that can strike anyone at any time and, although only lasting for a short time, bring with it an absolute conviction of its reality.

According to Dr Bucke, cosmic consciousness demonstrates that the cosmos does not consist of dead matter governed by unconscious, rigid, and unintending law. 'It shows it on the contrary as entirely immaterial, entirely spiritual and entirely alive; it shows that death is an absurdity, that everyone and everything has eternal life. It shows that the universe is God and that God is the universe, and that no evil ever did or ever will enter into it.'

Try it now	At this stage of your quest can you feel that you are:
	◆ An integral part of the planet?
	◆ An integral part of the universe?
	◆ An integral part of creation?

Although these experiences are fleeting, the seeker harbours no doubt of the reality of the sensation. We are being introduced to a totally new and different form of consciousness which we will find almost impossible to describe to those who have not shared a similar experience. This is where we often begin to separate from our family and friends who no longer understand the direction in which we are heading.

Rediscovering 'God'

However much we might like to deny it, God *is* out there. This may not be the divine presence of the religious textbooks but Marcus Chown, writing in *The Magic Furnace*, produces a more than reasonable argument for the existence of God from the *scientist's* point of view. In this extraordinary account of how modern science unravelled the mystery of atoms, we also learn that our bodies contain atoms 'forged in the blistering furnaces deep inside stars and blasted into space by stellar explosions that blazed brighter than a billion suns.'

Is this far-fetched science fiction? Not at all, for according to scientific data the iron in our blood, the calcium in our bones and the oxygen in our lungs contain atoms blown across unimaginable gulfs of space and time. Going back to ancient times, astrologers claimed that people's lives were ruled by the stars and as *The Magic Furnace* explains, they were right in essence if not in detail. Twentieth century science has discovered that we are far more intimately connected to events in the cosmos than anyone ever dared imagine, simply because those atoms that we carry around in our bodies originated in deep space.

These atoms were thrown out into space by the collapse of a giant star, adding to the swirling mass of gas and dust from which new stars were created. Eventually a cloud of gas and dust formed on the edge of the Milky Way, and in the cooling process the heavy elements in the cloud became incorporated into a new sun and its family of planets. In turn these elements became part of the Earth and ultimately the first primitive living cells . . . which means that 'every one of us was quite literally made in heaven. Each and every one of us is stardust made flesh.'

So scientific discovery compounds the mystical realisation of eternity and the state of 'deathlessness within oneself from which the whole universe of change and time and space is excluded.' If we comprise atoms that have been part of the cosmic ballet for

close on five billion years then the case for 'God' is surely proven.
We are no longer seeking amongst the doctrine and dogma of
organised religion but in the vast energy fields that exist in time
and space.

Towards the Discovery of Oneness

Our spiritual quest does not demand that we jettison religion as a
whole just because we now see things from a much wider
perspective. We must adopt a degree of amused tolerance when it
comes to the non-spiritual understanding of our fellows rather
than leaping onto a soap-box to share our newly discovered
wisdom.

Let us examine the approach of two articles that appeared
recently in the popular press. The first mooted the point often
raised by feminists who object to the idea of God being male. By
now the seeker will understand that God is neither male nor female
but an embodiment of both male and female attributes within the
Divine creative force. Even the Pope has publicly acknowledged
that God has both a male and female nature; remarks that were
welcomed by liberal theologians who believe that it's time to reveal
that the concept of God transcends the sexes.

The second referred to a report that warns Christians to avoid
healing therapies since the philosophies behind many healing
techniques such as reiki, yoga and shiatsu clash with Christianity.
A spokesman even went so far as to claim that 'some healing
techniques appeal to forces outside God . . .' which is rather
strange coming from a Christian organisation that believes its
God to be omnipotent and omnipresent. The true seeker,
however, knows there is no energy or force that is 'outside God'
since the divine creative spark is found in everything.

Unfortunately, the established religions do not take into
account that many in the congregation are no longer intellectually
stimulated by the myths and parables that have held them in
check for hundreds of years. When the priesthood was the only
educated class, it was necessary to introduce a plethora of saints
and lesser gods to act as a buffer between the brilliant splendour
of the Creator and the petitioner. In the modern world many now
demand more from their faith than dictum or dogma.

Pursuit of the Absolute

Our quest for spiritual growth will eventually lead us towards the mystical aspects of our own faith, whatever we perceive it to be. Here we should recall the subtle differences between the *kensho* and the *satori* experiences. According to some esoteric writers there are three distinct levels of mysticism, the first being cosmic consciousness. The second is the realisation of eternity and the true implications of the state of 'deathlessness' – that the 'soul' cannot die. The third is the union of the soul with the absolute.

The absolute is commonly referred to as the One and we are all an essential part of the One. This means that our inner-most self is identical with the absolute with its unchanging power against a backdrop of the changing universe. This means that we do not live solely within our own lives, but within the life of the universe, which has its foundation in a changeless being; which is at the same time one's own eternity. Therefore, although the seeker is aware of the One behind the many faces of deity, we can still feel ourselves to be an integral part of that Oneness. This is simply because all things come together in the One just as spokes form a bridge between the rim and the hub of a wheel – and the wheel is a universal symbol of spiritual harmony.

The following is part of a prayer that may sum up the seeker's perspective on the inscrutable, omnipotent and omniscient Creator – but you may be surprised at its origins:

Alone, without a second.
One, the maker of all things,
The spirit, the hidden spirit, the maker of spirits.
He existed in the beginning, when nothing else was.
What is he created after he came into being.
Father of beginnings, eternal, infinite, ever-lasting.
Hidden One, no man knoweth his form,
Or can search out his likeness;
He is hidden to gods and men,
And is a mystery to his creatures.
No man knoweth how to know him;
His name is a mystery and hidden.

(Ancient Egyptian)

Although the ancient Egyptians worshipped a pantheon comprising hundreds of deities, they were very conscious of the All-Seeing One, the Being, the One Alone, who was regarded as invisible. No artist or sculptor ever made any representation of him even in a culture that was highly graphic with images of its gods, which indicates how spiritually advanced they were all those thousands of years ago.

We Shall Not Cease from Our Exploration

As the Bishop of Edinburgh commented: 'The trouble with life is that we understand it backwards, but have to live it forwards. We keep moving through life trying to figure it out as we go along, living experimentally, trying out different attitudes and theories, changing our minds, reversing ourselves, sometimes coming back to where we were at the beginning.'

Perhaps it makes it easier if we accept that there are three types of religious/spiritual experience:

◆ The **ancient rites** are essentially of a propitiatory nature and designed to deflect the anger of a deity, or attract their benevolence.
◆ **The mysteries** purge the soul and allow us to glimpse eternity, often through unity with the deity.
◆ **Philosophy** attempts not to simply define the material world (through explanation, myth, taboo, etc.) but suggests practical ways to the 'good life'.

When we began this journey together we looked at the problems and difficulties that were strewn across the path to hamper our progress. By encouraging an inward look at ourselves and our motives for undertaking the quest, we began the process of self-cultivation. Hopefully our quality of life and relationships have shown a marked improvement since we took control of them. Without having solid foundations on which to build, however, the whole quest would be in danger of crumbling away at the slightest challenge.

Try it now   You have begun to develop the inner strength to face the challenge. How do you now feel about the following:

◆ Are you more willing to accept responsibility for your actions?

- ◆ Do you feel more relaxed about being part of the indefinable?
- ◆ Do you feel a greater sense of balance and commitment?

You may have already set out on a different path to the one you expected to take. Others may have taken the 'pretty way' in order to admire the scenery before completing the journey back to where they started – only this time they can view their faith with a new understanding. Or you may have followed that gut feeling that's been tugging at you for years. Whichever path we find ourselves taking, our minds will remain open and free from prejudice and misinformation; rich in the understanding that all paths are valid and all, ultimately, help us find our way back to the Creator, who or whatever we perceive it to be.

Case Study

If you are going to commit yourself completely to a spiritual path and ultimately aim for the priesthood, either ordained or in a lay capacity, you will be required to take an oath to serve your deity in the manner prescribed by your tradition. Many take this oath as a means to an end, to obtain power over others. When this power is used to abuse a position of trust, then the oath is broken, no matter what justification is raised for the priest's actions.

Derek took his vows as a priest and established his own teaching group that built up an impressive following within a very short space of time. Unfortunately, as the group grew in strength, so did Derek's ego and he began imposing his own rules and codes of conduct on members. There were the occasional whispers of sexual impropriety and on several occasions he was formally reprimanded by elders of the priesthood. Developing a power complex he singled out 'favourites' for special privileges, but if they failed to bend to his will they would find themselves ostracised as a means of bringing them to heel. The group members soon discovered that they could no longer rely on him.

Derek broke just about every oath he made – and then it all started going wrong. His marriage failed and, along with his health, his financial situation bordered upon precarious. His enemies began actively campaigning against him and when he complained to the elders they tried to explain that he'd brought all his woes down on his own head by betraying the oath he'd made to his deity. A period of mediation and meditation was recommended but Derek refused to accept any responsibility for his actions, placing blame everywhere but on himself.

In the end he said he was sick of the lot of them and that he was finished with everything, including his deity. But as one of the elders remarked when he'd slammed out of the door: 'He might be finished with the Gods, but have they finished with *him!*' _____

Summary

Before you close this book for the last time, go back to the beginning and compare the responses you made in your journal. Ask yourself the same questions and, where the answers are different, record your new reaction in a different coloured pen underneath the original remarks. As we said at the beginning, this isn't a book about religion, it's a book about you . . . your hopes, your dreams and your aspirations. Only you can make the decision about which path you wish to tread. If you feel that you wish to remain with your original faith, then we hope you will be able to look at it through a more discerning pair of eyes.

For those who wish to follow a different path we hope we have given you enough information to be able to ask the right questions to follow your quest to its natural conclusion. The next part of the journey is for you to take on your own, wherever it will lead.

All that is left is silence and a finger pointing the way.

> We shall not cease from our exploration
> And at the end of all our exploring
> Will be to arrive where we started
> And know the place for the first time.

(Little Gidding – T S Eliot)

Further Reading and Listening

Recommended Reading

Ancient Wisdom, Modern World, HH the Dalai Lama (Little, Brown, 1999).

Aromatherapy an A–Z, Patricia Davis (C W Daniel, 1999).

The Art of Happiness, HH the Dalai Lama and Howard C Cutler (Hodder & Stoughton, 1998).

Godless Morality, Richard Holloway, Bishop of Edinburgh (Canongate, 1999).

Intelligent Emotion, Frances Wilks (Arrow, 1998).

The Magic Furnace, Marcus Chown (Jonathon Cape, 1999).

Men Are from Mars, Women Are from Venus, John Gray (Thorsons, 1993).

The New Believers, David V Barrett (Cassell, 2001).

Take Time for Your Life, Cheryl Richardson (Bantam, 2000).

What You Call Time, Suzanne Ruthven (ignotus press, 1998).

The World's Religions, Ninian Smart (Cambridge University Press, 1998).

Recommended Listening

Music to create a meditational atmosphere

Pachalbel: Canon in D.

Enya: Boudicca (The Celts album).

Spiritual atmosphere

Albinoni: Adagio in G minor.

Fauré: Paradisium from Requiem.

Strauss: Transfiguration from Death and Transfiguration.

Gounod: Offertory, Sanctus from St Celia Mass.

Holst: Neptune, the Mystic, from The Planets.

Wagner: Prelude to Act 1 from Lohengrin.

Gregorian chant.

Dreamy atmosphere

Debussy: *Prelude to the Afternoon of a Fawn.*
Dvorak: *Largo* from *New World Symphony*, 2nd movement.
Adiemus: *Amate Adea.*
Holst: *Saturn, Bringer of Old Age*, from *The Planets.*
Selected tracks from Clannad.
Maire Brennan: *Ce Leis (Maire).*
Arnold Bax: *The Happy Forest.*

Playful atmosphere

Vaughan Williams: *Fantasia on a Theme by Thomas Tallis.*
Villa-Lobos: *Bachianas Brasilleras #5.*
Tchaikovsky: *Scherzo* from *Symphony #4.*
Holst: *Mercury, Winged Messenger*, from *The Planets.*
Marie Brennan: *Oro (Maire).*

Exciting atmosphere

Mussorgski-Ravel: *Great Gate at Kiev*, from *Pictures at an Exhibition.*
Holst: *Mars, Bringer of War*, from *The Planets.*
Clinka: *Aria* from *Ivan Susanin*, Act IV.
Maire Brennan: *Against the Wind (Maire).*

Vigorous atmosphere

Wagner: *The Ride of the Valkyries* from *Die Walkure.*
Respighi: *I pini della Via Appia, Pini di Roma (Pines of Rome).*
Orf: *Carmina Burana (O Fortuna).*

Healing/soothing atmosphere

Gentle flowing harp music (*The Healing Harp*).
Plainchant.

Useful Addresses

The Buddhist Society. For information about Buddhist activities in the UK contact to The Buddhist Society, 58 Eccleston Square, London SW1V 1PH. Tel: (020) 7834 5858.

Corvus Books. Produces a whole series of booklets and fact sheets on all aspects of pagan belief. Send a first class stamp to Corvus Books, 17 Melton Fields, Brickyard Lane, North Ferriby, East Yorkshire HU14 3HE.

Feasac Press. For a booklist covering the indigenous Traditions of the British Isles send a first class stamp to Feasac Press, 83 Rosslyn Road, Whitwick, Leicestershire LE67 5PU.

New World Music. Here you will find the most amazing collection of ethnic and natural music guaranteed to send you off into another world. Send two first class stamps for a catalogue from New World Music Limited, The Barn, Backs Green Lane, Ilketshall St Andrews, Beccles, Suffolk NR34 8PD.

Pathfinder. The authors of *Exploring Spirituality* appreciate that this book will provoke more questions than it answers. Whereas they cannot guarantee an answer for every letter, attempts will be made to forward enquiries to someone qualified to respond. Send letter with SAE to ignotus press (Dept PATH), BCM-Writer, London WC1N 3XX.

Raven. For a wide range of candles, joss sticks, evaporators and essential oils at reasonable prices, send two first class stamps to Raven at 17 Melton Fields, Brickyard Lane, North Ferruby, Hull HU14 3NE.

SPCK Bookshops (Society for Promoting Christian Knowledge). Branches throughout the UK that offer a range of both Christian and non-Christian books. If there isn't a branch in your local telephone directory contact The SPCK Bookshop, Holy Trinity Church, Marylebone Road, London NW1 4SU. Tel: (020) 7387 5282.

Index